RUNNING AGAINST THE ODDS

RUNNING AGAINST THE ODDS

AN INSPIRATIONAL JOURNEY TO MAKING HIGH SCHOOL SPORTS HISTORY

DESMOND DUNHAM

FOREWORD BY MARCUS O'SULLIVAN

RUNNING AGAINST THE ODDS

An Inspirational Journey to Making High School Sports History

ISBN   978-1-63676-487-0   *Paperback*

            978-1-63730-397-9   *Kindle Ebook*

            978-1-63730-398-6   *Ebook*

For my mother, Helen Dunham, who loves me unconditionally and taught me what sacrifice for your family and for others really means.

For my father, Ted Dunham, who fought for our country, who never got a chance to benefit from a mother's nurturing love, and whose shortcomings as a father became an impetus for me to strive to disrupt the cycle.

For my wife, Jami Dunham, and children, Niles and Nia Dunham, who have supported me in this journey and who are the reason for it all. Without you, none of this would be possible.

And for the ones who think the odds are insurmountable, keep on running onward and upward.

CONTENTS

FOREWORD

I met Desmond Dunham for the first time some twenty years ago when he arrived mid-August to RunningWorks, a camp for high school cross country runners. At the time, I remember thinking his team was composed mostly of sprinters, and it struck me as odd that he would subject them to the gruels of cross country running. I came to realize during that week at camp that the young runners from Eleanor Roosevelt High School in Greenbelt, Maryland, had the deepest respect for their coach and were simply happy to be there with him.

Over the years, Desmond attended many of my coaching clinics. A distance runner since high school, Desmond was always committed to cross country himself and went on to lead Eleanor Roosevelt to national acclaim both in cross country and track. Unorthodox as it may have been, he was committed to learning as much about the aerobic system as he could, and he believed in its importance in the development of his short and long sprinters.

If you ever have the opportunity to meet Desmond, he will immediately engage you. Disarmingly soft-spoken, you quickly realize his intensity and genuine passion for coaching. His devotion to his athletes is centered around the whole person, providing them with structure, emphasizing dedication, and above all else, leading with much needed care and kindness. He is an enthusiastic man full of curiosity in his search to become a better coach and has an insatiable appetite for knowledge. His work ethic is second to none and, therefore, the foundation of what makes him a great, tenacious coach.

What I saw twenty years ago was just a sliver of who Desmond really is. His journey is revealed in this book. It is a coming-of-age story about growing up in Gary, Indiana, the once vibrant city of the early 1960s. With the failing steel industry, the city began to quickly decompose, and by the late '80s, it had fully transformed from being the Magic City to the Murder Capital of America, infested with drugs and gangs. Devoid of a consistent and positive father figure in his home, Desmond learned to navigate life and came to the realization that he could be a better version of himself, despite the numerous challenges brought on by his circumstances. Predominately Black, Gary was a segregated city, a classic example of America's systemic racism conveniently overlooked. Desmond's journey was more doomed for failure than success from the start. Fortunately, he found the sport of cross country, and it forever changed his life. He encountered two very important coaches along the way who continued to help shape him to become the person he is today. You do become your influences, both the good and the bad. However, you have a choice. This is the story of Desmond's choice. His positive attitude was tested often, with setbacks and disappointments, yet he overcame all odds, ultimately recognizing that he lives in an imperfect and unjust world but that it simply cannot be his reason for failure.

Each chapter is layered on the last with valuable and insightful lessons. Desmond innately gravitates toward helping others and through education and coaching creates a positive environment for America's often marginalized youth to survive, grow, and prosper. His meaningful life can be an inspiration to everyone. Yes, Desmond's book includes wonderfully depicted races culminating with the Penn Relays. But, most importantly, you will witness how one individual, through his own personal journey, can make such a profound difference in the lives of others.

—MARCUS O'SULLIVAN

VILLANOVA UNIVERSITY MEN'S TRACK AND FIELD &

CROSS COUNTRY HEAD COACH, FOUR-TIME OLYMPIAN

AUTHOR'S NOTE

—

"You've probably heard the saying that nothing in life is certain except death and taxes. You could almost throw in Jamaican dominance at Penns, too!"

Those words from writer and track enthusiast Tim Fulton were challenged on that momentous Friday, April 27, 2007. We had come to accomplish the unthinkable.

The scene was set. Over thirty-nine thousand fans were in attendance, with thousands more livestreaming, to witness the much-anticipated Jamaica versus USA showdown. We were at one of the most historic track meets in the world—the Super Bowl of high school track and field meets—the 113th Penn Relays Carnival. I was the coach of a girls track and field team from Greenbelt, Maryland, representing the USA against the dominant Jamaican runners.

After nearly a three-hour delay due to lightning and heavy rainfall, the starter's gun finally fired to signal the beginning of the race. The crowd immediately began to roar, chanting: "U-S-A! Ja-mai-ca! U-S-A! Ja-mai-ca!" Green, black, and gold flags waved vigorously throughout the stadium. Whistles shrieked boldly and consistently. It was reminiscent of an ancient gladiator scene in which the crowd anxiously waits to see who will stand victorious after an all-out battle. It was a nail-biter from start to finish with the top two teams—my team from Eleanor Roosevelt High School and their team from Holmwood Technical High School of Christiana, Jamaica—laboriously matching each other, stride for stride, back and forth, until the final steps across the finish line.

If we won, this feat would be more than just a victory; it would forever change these young runners' lives. It would be a lesson in continuing to fight for what you believe in, despite hardship and setback. Even me standing in that very stadium was a testament to my humble beginnings.

I am from Gary, Indiana, a city that thrived economically after the Great Migration of more than six million African Americans from the rural South to the cities of the North, Midwest, and West in the 1960s and '70s. But for anyone who grew up in the city during the 1970s and '80s, the bustling industry and opportunities within the predominantly Black city had deteriorated, lagging significantly behind its neighboring cities. Many people in America believe in meritocracy, that all we need to do to succeed is work hard and pull ourselves up by our bootstraps. From my childhood, I learned some of us don't get boots in the first place.

Growing up in Gary, we all had to overcome a duality of love and community, coupled with trauma and challenge. I lost three childhood friends who grew up on my block to homicides. By the 1990s, Gary had become the murder capital of the United States (per capita). (Sloan, 1994) We lacked educational resources, dealt with limited employment opportunities, and managed without the safety and security enjoyed by surrounding suburbs and those beyond. Despite those circumstances, I had amazing childhood experiences. Nothing could replace playing in homemade, organized "sandlot" neighborhood sports leagues with my buddies, or attending nurturing, fun-filled annual reunions with my Wilson and Dunham families.

Yet all memories were layered with the inevitable vices of my home city. My darkest moments involve experiences with my dad and his iniquities. Like many veterans, he did not get the support he needed, and he suffered for it. And so did I.

My childhood trauma is not unique. Sadly, so many share my experiences—an alcoholic parent, domestic abuse, urban violence—or even more desperate circumstances. But for many, unfortunately, their dreams are never realized. Sports became my outlet, and running changed the trajectory of my life for the better.

I was compelled to write this book in the hopes that the events that led to that 2007 victory would inspire others to continue their own race despite the odds stacked against them. In this book, I share the disappointments and rejections that preceded my triumphs in running and, ultimately, led to my unexpectedly vibrant career as a coach. If you have ever felt like an underdog with something inside that wouldn't let you quit, then this book is for you. The way we run life's race can alter our ability to successfully overcome inevitable adversity. I hope this book inspires you to keep running forward, always.

PART I

CHILDHOOD

*If you want to know the end,
look at the beginning.*

—AFRICAN PROVERB

CHAPTER 1

THE WARMUP

"Alright boys! This is your time to show me whatcha got. Now, this is cross country, so for those of you who don't like to run—this ain't the sport for you!" Coach Robinson said with emphasis and a slight chuckle. "You have one moderate run today. If you can keep up with the pack, you might make the team. If you stop, you're cut. Now, on the line!"

As a kid, I had serious hoop dreams. So, when the fall of my seventh-grade year rolled around, I was willing to do whatever it took to make the boys basketball team. All my buddies told me I had to play football or run cross country to increase my chances of making the team, so to make my dream a reality, I went out for cross country. And it was a complete disaster.

We shuffled off the bleachers and hustled to the starting line.

No one told me you run slower when you have one hand on your side nursing a cramp while trying to negotiate leverage and balance with one determined arm left pumping. But that is exactly what I looked like after mile one of three. Nearing mile two, I thought, *Maybe it was a bad idea to stuff a footlong hot dog down just before practice.* My chest was burning, and my legs soon followed, but my stomach and the urge to vomit felt ten times worse. Each breath provided comfort, affirming I was in fact still alive, but also brought pain as the gulps of dry air felt like needles going down my parched throat. *Oh no, should I stop and get my inhaler?* I knew I could easily trigger my asthma, but Coach Robinson's voice echoed in my head: "If you stop, you're cut!"

Four laps around the track, then a neighborhood two-mile loop was pure agony.

"How much longer?" I asked the guys near me after the second mile and a half. No one responded. "How much longer?" I asked, this time as loud as I could muster.

Finally someone replied, "Dude, shut up and run!"

I felt the lactic acid eating away at my muscle tissue. My legs were swimming. I did not pace the first mile and thought if I ran faster in the beginning, I could put myself out front, and then I could slow down and run just fast enough to still finish among the top runners. My plan thoroughly failed. I stumbled across the finish line, gasping for air, and collapsed to my knees. Even the desperate puffs from my inhaler didn't ease the tension from my chest until well after the run was over.

I showed up to the second day of tryouts with a different strategy. I hadn't recovered from the previous day, so I decided to hang out in the back of the pack for a less painful run. I coasted and did just enough not to be last.

The next day, Coach Robinson posted the new team list on the locker room door. I scanned down the list hoping to see my name. It was not there.

I'm not surprised, I thought. *My asthma is too bad for me to run anyway.* My pediatrician, Dr. Simpson, had always warned that sports could be even more of a challenge for me because of the extra effort my lungs had to make to breathe under stress. But the rejection and failure still stung. I wanted to make the team, and I was unsettled by my efforts. I knew I had more in me.

* * *

Frankly, I wasn't supposed to survive, let alone amount to anything worth noting.

I was born with a respiratory infection on July 19, 1972, in Gary. My birth foreshadowed truths I would grow to learn about my life—nothing would come easily to me, and my victories would be possible only because of the struggles that preceded them.

My mother's water broke early on that Wednesday morning. She was alone in the apartment, frantically phoning my dad's brothers Hank and John in an attempt to reach him.

"Oh, Lord," she cried out. "This baby is coming!" As she contemplated who else to call, the realization that she couldn't wait much longer settled in.

She opened the apartment door and cautiously walked cradling her belly. Managing to totter a few feet, she knocked on the adjacent apartment's door yelling, "Shirley!"

Thank goodness her sister lived next door in the Westbrook Apartments. My Aunt Shirley quickly got dressed and came over to help my mother toss a few items in a bag. As a seasoned licensed practical nurse, Aunt Shirley was the perfect person to assist my mom in this crisis.

They left my dad a note and quickly made their way to Methodist Hospital. My mother did her best to convince her prenatal nurse I was on my way much sooner than expected— the nurse did not heed my mom's urgent warning.

"I'm telling you my baby is coming out now!" my mom exclaimed.

"Ma'am, you're not dilated enough," replied the nurse. "Your baby is probably not going to come anytime soon. Your contractions are not close enough."

My mom huffed. She was baffled, and although she didn't agree with the nurse, she didn't argue. By this point, my dad had gotten word and made it to the hospital. Anticipating he had plenty of time based on the nurse's response, he headed to the cafeteria to grab a snack. Within minutes of his absence, my mother suddenly slumped over and shrieked in pain, "He's coming!" She had been in labor just a year before with my sister, so she recognized the feelings and contortions intimately.

The nurse still held her ground and said, "Ma'am, you will be fine. Just calm down and try to relax. Your baby isn't coming this fast. You have a long labor ahead of you." Though off-duty, my aunt worked at this hospital and decided it was time to pull rank.

"She needs to be re-examined right now," Aunt Shirley demanded.

With a deep sigh, the nurse grabbed another set of gloves and a mask. After a quick peek, her eyes widened in shock as she realized my head was crowning. She quickly vacated the examination room to inform her medical team and ordered them to prepare a delivery room immediately. They rushed my mother to the next room and encouraged her to calm down to give time for the doctor to arrive, but clearly, I had already made up my mind. I was delivered in just under thirty minutes.

My dad returned from his snack in the nick of time to witness and support my delivery but left shortly afterward to get some sleep after his long night out on the town on the eve of my birth. This would be just the first of many moments when his fast life kept him away from our family.

After my mother's sedation wore off, she was eager to see and hold me. The nurses, however, whisked me away before she had a chance.

"Where's my baby?" she asked anxiously. The nurses were evasive in their responses. Finally, the doctor came back into the room to explain I had been born with a respiratory infection and that the first twenty-four hours of my life were extremely critical. I was diagnosed with respiratory distress syndrome, which results in labored breathing, underdeveloped lungs, and discolored skin. Born about a month premature, I was in a fight for my life. The first time my mother would see me would be through a big glass window as I labored to breathe through an oxygen tent.

My amazing mom, Helen Joyce Dunham (née Wilson), spent the rest of the night crying and praying with the other new mother with whom she shared a hospital room. This prayer, along with countless others, would be sent up that night and almost every night of my life. My mom's prayers mirrored so many Black mothers who raise sons growing up in cities like Gary.

The next morning, the doctor informed my mother that things were looking up for me. Yet, she spent the first week of my life visiting me from behind a glass window. It would end up being eight long days until she held me in her arms for the first time. I spent another week at the hospital, where Aunt Shirley kept an extra eye on me during her shifts, before I was released to go home.

Though I had cleared this initial medical hurdle, I found myself facing another one less than six months later. In a routine checkup, my doctor realized many of my sleepless nights and crying were because of a hernia. The doctor was afraid that if my bowel did not retreat back into my abdomen, it could get stuck in the strangulated part of my stomach, then swell and burst. At that appointment, my pediatrician advised my mom to readmit me to the hospital. I was rushed to surgery. My mother paced the lobby floors, praying and crying, waves of guilt washing over her. A year earlier, when she learned she was pregnant again just four months after my sister was born, she had been less than elated. She was a sleep-deprived new mother, and the thought of another baby—me—was overwhelming. As she waited during my surgery, she wondered whether her initial reaction to her second pregnancy somehow caused my health challenges.

The cycle of worry continued throughout the three hours I was in surgery. The pediatric surgeon emerged into the lobby and assured my mom I would heal just fine. For the second time in my short life, I overcame a major medical challenge. And once again, my mother's prayers prevailed.

CHAPTER 2

THE STARTING LINE

———

"Daddy, did you do this all the time with your dad, too?" Niles asked.

"You know what, Niles?" I replied, "I never ever caught a ball from my dad. Not once."

As a kid, my dad was around but not present in my home or daily life. Decades later, while tossing a baseball with my eleven-year-old son, Niles, I shared stories about my childhood, which was significantly different from his.

"What do you mean?" Niles asked. "Was he sick?"

The idea that my dad and I never spent time doing what Niles and I did together so often was inconceivable to him. For Niles, it was routine. He didn't understand why a dad would choose to spend time doing anything else.

It was such a paradox—the countless hours Niles and I spent together and the fact that I did not have a single memory of doing the same with my own dad.

My dad, Theodore Dunham Jr., was born January 31, 1942, in Lillybrook, West Virginia. He was one of nine siblings who his parents had together and one of ten on his father's side. Besides sharing a name and similar good looks, my dad and his father shared a love of "hanging out."

As a young man, my dad grew to be tall and slender, and with his caramel complexion, chiseled cheekbones, and dark brown eyes, he was quite a catch. Though my dad and his siblings were close and our extended families often got together for Friday fish fries and Sunday dinners, it was clear he was happier when he could just hang out, drink, and play cards rather than be a responsible and supportive parent. Gambling, drinking, and philandering became vices my father couldn't quite control.

Growing up, your home is supposed to be a safe place. For much of my childhood, my home was not. I often felt anxious, never knowing when something was about to erupt. My dad was always the igniter. When he wasn't there, it was quiet and peaceful. When he was there, it was all ablaze. I never had time to run for cover.

One hot summer day, for example, my dad came staggering out of the car while my older sister Nikki (whom I affectionately nicknamed "Shnicks") and I were playing out front with some friends. As always, there was no warning before the chaos flared.

"Whachall doin' on da grass? Alllways . . . try'na mess up . . . shit. . . . Come ova here. . . ." My dad's words slurred as he approached us, and we bolted toward the house in hopes of avoiding any further embarrassment.

My mother, who was sitting on the front porch, jumped up and started toward my dad, hoping to de-escalate him.

"Now, Ted, the kids are just playin'," she started as she continued to walk toward him.

"Helen, what the hell do you want? Get away from me!" he interrupted her. A few neighbors outside on this warm spring day began to look in their direction. Our friends slowly eased out of our yard.

"Ted, leave the kids alone! You're drunk. Now go in the house and lay down," my mother urged.

Shnicks and I braced behind our mother.

"Who the hell you talkin' to, Helen?" he barked as he grabbed her arms.

"Stop, Daddy!" Shnicks begged him. "Let Mama go!"

But it was too late. He was focused on our mother as his problem, and he wouldn't let her go. As our mother twisted and attempted to turn and step back, there was a loud blaring honk from the street.

We turned in the direction of the noise as a black car rolled down our street, coming closer to our house, then abruptly stopped and parked. The door opened, and my Aunt Barbara emerged. Aunt Barbara was my dad's youngest sister, who lived a few blocks away. Leaving the keys in the ignition and the driver's side door open, she hustled quickly to my parents and jumped between my mom and dad.

Standing at least a foot shorter than my dad, Aunt Barbara looked up and pleaded, "Come on, Ted, not here. Not here, Ted. Let's go in and talk about it. Come on in the house. Come on now, not in front of the kids."

My dad mumbled something inaudible and began to stumble toward the house, with my Aunt Barbara pulling him gently away from my mom. I knew my dad had the utmost respect for his siblings, and my Aunt Barbara settled for nothing less. I felt humiliated by this public display of our dysfunction.

Once my dad was passed out on the couch, my aunt loaded me and Shnicks in her car and took us to her house for a peaceful reprieve away from the madness. It wasn't the first, and it surely wouldn't be the last time she would help us escape and find some rare moments of tranquility.

My father was supposed to validate my masculinity and manhood, to instill a sense of value, to provide for our family emotionally and financially. He was supposed to be a gate-keeper, to make our home a refuge. He was supposed to be home in time for dinner, to ask me about my day, and to throw a baseball with me in the front yard. He was supposed to show me how to tie a tie, how to shave, and how to ask a girl out on a date. Shnicks and I would learn and come to believe he loved us. But in those early days, we were often either afraid or embarrassed by his actions, and we routinely prayed for normalcy in our home.

I was about twelve years old when I learned that my dad's mother died shortly after childbirth with her ninth child. My dad was only five years old when she passed away. I'll never know why he lacked the ability to be a good father to any of his kids, but I often wonder what had the biggest impact. Was it losing his mother at such a young age? Was it his own father's struggle to raise nine kids? Was it the death and violence he experienced firsthand in Vietnam? Was it the stress of the blue-collar work he did at the Inland Steel Company, which eventually led him to abuse alcohol? Was it the racism that so pervasively confronted young Black men in Gary and in so many other American cities and towns?

I never had a conversation with my dad about his experience in the war, but my mother told me that he was not the same person when he returned as when he departed. She noted that before he left for his two-year tour of duty, he was quiet but full of spirit. He was artistic and liked to draw. He was fun to be around, and he had even created a singing group with two of his brothers. Of course, he was the lead singer and called all of the shots. But when he returned from the war, he was more withdrawn. He mostly avoided talking about his experiences in combat. He did share with my mom that one of his assignments was to pick up wounded and dead bodies from the battlefield. Could anyone avoid being changed by spending so much time with death? My dad grew up during a time when mental health was not openly discussed or prioritized, especially for veterans. So many young people fought and were forever changed, only to return home with little to no support or resources to heal the physical, mental, and emotional scars that the war left. And you simply didn't talk about it.

An additional layer of challenge that my dad faced coming home after the war was the ever-present racism. I can only imagine the kind of rejection and humiliation he felt, like so many vets, when he returned and found that the country he fought for continued to dehumanize him and not support his mental rehabilitation. In addition, the US Department of Veterans Affairs' benefits, like low interest rates for loans for new homes, that his White counterparts enjoyed weren't offered to Black veterans, at least not in Gary. He came home knowing that regardless of how many Americans he had protected in Vietnam, he as a Black man would not be respected or protected in America.

As a kid, I didn't have the language to describe my dad's mood swings, his volatility, his tendency to choose bars and bottles over my baseball games and spelling bees. He treated the reality of parenthood and adulthood the same way. As an adult, I now realize my dad probably suffered from post-traumatic stress disorder (PTSD), anxiety, and depression, which heightened his desire to escape from his harsh realities and into his addictions. Instead of counseling and intensive therapy, my dad self-medicated with gin, vodka, bid whist, and poker.

While I wondered about my father's experiences and his coping mechanisms, I was well into adulthood before I ever asked about my parents' love story. Not even when I took my own walk down the aisle did I think to ask how they fell in love. When I finally did ask my mom how she and my dad met, the story was as complex as I could have imagined.

"We first met in summer school," she told me. "I was sixteen, and I thought he was really handsome and nice."

No sparks flew in the hallways of Roosevelt High School during that hot summer of 1958. But five years later, my mom saw my dad again, at a party, after his tour of duty in Vietnam.

"I was really smitten by him. He was tall and quiet but confident. I liked that about him," she reminisced.

Even though she knew my dad already had a daughter named Deneen and that he was not present in her life, my mother could not resist his tall and slender charm. She was once warned by another young lady to be careful because he had eyes for many women. At the time, my mother did not appreciate that advice.

After my parents were married, my mother saw much more—other women, a son named Darin born shortly after their marriage to the same mother as Deneen, gambling, drinking, and a flaring temper that often resulted in physical and emotional abuse. In their first year of marriage, my parents led the life of a typical couple in the 1970s, attending concerts, dinners, house parties, family gatherings, and other social events. By the time they settled into their 500-square-foot attached Westbrook apartment, it began to go downhill. My mom grew fearful of my dad anytime he began to drink. The stress and abuse escalated while she was pregnant with me. It was so intense that at times, Aunt Shirley would intervene, getting in the line of fire herself.

I was nine years old when my dad was forced to acknowledge his two oldest children. Darin and Deneen were both in the bank cashing their summer work checks. Darin was fifteen and Deneen was seventeen. Darin, tall and slim like my dad, stood with his mother on one side of the bank, and Deneen waited in another line on the other side of the bank with a friend. Before my dad could bolt the other way, he made eye contact with Darin's mother, Dee. My dad was forced to face the inevitable. Wearing a beige straw hat, a short-sleeve silk shirt, slacks, and dress shoes, my dad walked up to Dee.

She turned to my brother and said, "Darin, this is your father." Darin was caught off guard and completely surprised by the introduction to the stranger. After a brief handshake and failed attempt at conversation, our dad quickly and uncomfortably exchanged numbers with Dee.

As our dad walked away, Dee mentioned that Deneen was on the other side of the bank, but his nerves got the best of him. He quickly headed to the exit, mumbling something about calling her later. I am certain he did not anticipate running into his children that day. He had not seen Deneen since she was two years old, though they lived less than a mile away from us.

A couple of weeks after he saw Deneen and Darin in the bank, my dad announced to me and Shnicks that we had two older siblings.

"They're coming over here today so y'all can meet them," he said.

"What're their names?" I asked. At that age, learning I had siblings was exciting.

When they walked in the house, I initially just stood there, amazed at how much my brother looked like my dad. Same build and complexion, similar sleepy eyes, and carbon-copy sharp jawbone. After all the years of failed attempts to get my sister to wrestle and tussle with me, I actually had a big brother I could roughhouse with. After a minute or so, I jumped on Darin like he was a jungle gym.

It was a weird dynamic in the beginning. They were strangers, but I was happy to have more playmates. My mom didn't say much. As I got older, I noticed how she would retreat when they were around. I think they reminded her of my dad's unwillingness and inability to truly be committed to his family. I'm sure Dee felt the same. It was easier for my mom to pretend the betrayals didn't exist. She never blamed Darin and Deneen, but to say we became one big, happy, blended family was far from the truth.

We worked on building a bond that would have been there naturally if we had grown up together. Despite the resentment and pain my dad caused all of us, we learned to love one another.

Many years later, my sister Deneen told me something that tugged hard at my heart.

"I wrote Daddy a letter every year on my birthday until my senior year in high school. In those letters, I would tell him that all I wanted as a birthday gift was to see him," she relayed to me on an emotional phone call. "And to know that he had the chance in the bank that day to meet me and he chose not to just crushed me."

He never acknowledged Deneen and Darin in their childhood. Deneen rightfully felt jealous of the perceived privileged family life that Shnicks and I had. But my dad's presence didn't feel like a gift at all.

What Deneen didn't see were my dad's rants escalating at home. We had friends who witnessed these tirades. Many went back and told others at the school, and we were the topic of embarrassing gossip around the school and neighborhood. One of these rants led to my mom, Shnicks, and me fleeing the house to find safety with my maternal grandmother, whom we grew up affectionately calling Mama Hattie. My dad went after my mom. The confrontation intensified when he arrived, escalating all the adults to a screaming match.

"Get outta here, Ted! You're drunk and you actin' crazy!" my mom shrieked.

"Shut up Helen! Who you think you talkin' to? You keep pissin' me off an' makin' me mad. You an' da kids betta . . ."

"She said get outta here!" Mama Hattie interjected.

"I ain't goin' nowhere wit' out 'dem! Come on here, Helen!" My dad's rage continued to spiral as he staggered closer. "You know I ain't playin' wit' you, an' you know what I'll do if you keep doin' dis shit!"

As my dad continued to threaten my mother, Mama Hattie quickly ran into her room and came back with one hand behind her back.

"Ted, I dare you to take one more step t'ward us," she said with an intense and daring look in her eyes. "You wanna live to see another day, you best walk back out that door!"

Without another word, my dad retreated, turned, and left.

My mother said in relief, "I didn't know you had a gun Mama."

Mama Hattie replied, "I don't," and then showed my mother her empty hand. They both smiled and embraced to console one another. They both knew my mom was enduring the abuse for the sake of her kids.

Many times, my dad became abusive after my mother inquired about why he didn't return home after paydays, why he so often disappeared for days at a time. In one such incident, my mother anxiously greeted my dad as he came through the front door, directing him to continue the conversation in the living room. Shnicks and I positioned ourselves at the top of the stairs to listen. My mom's temper and my dad's defensiveness only grew.

"Where have you been, Ted? We need groceries. What are we going to do without your check?"

"Don't question me! It's my life and my money, Helen! Leave me alone, dammit!" The intensity of his voice made my insides quiver.

"Well, what are we supposed to do about money? We need to buy groceries, and we can't have the lights cut off! We have kids, and they can't live like this!" my mom continued. Instinctively, my sister put her arm over my shoulder.

"Just shut up, okay? I don't need you on my back about this. I know what I'm doin'. I don't need you tellin' me what to do!"

Frustrated and disgusted, my mom attempted to walk away. My dad blocked her path and made it clear he called his own shots.

"This is my muthafuc--n' house, you hear me?! Shit, you don't tell me what to do!"

His retorts escalated as he hurled curse after curse, followed by a push, and then finally he launched a lamp, then a shoe, and, finally, he pushed over a chair. Shnicks and I retreated to my sister's room upstairs, hugging each other tightly, so afraid and helpless. We silently prayed that in spite of the crying and screams, my mother was okay.

Years later as an adult, I asked my mother how many times my dad hit her. She responded, "It happened so much I lost count." Despite justifiable reasons for my mother to confront my father, these confrontations always backfired, causing her to be scolded for simply trying to hold him accountable.

CHAPTER 3

MAN OF THE HOUSE

———

My father's drunken behavior was as normal to me during my childhood as watching cartoons on Saturday mornings. He was a gin drinker, so you couldn't smell the alcohol, and he would often hide bottles around the house that Shnicks would eventually find. He would hide them in the toilet water tank, the lazy Susan in the kitchen, and behind the couches in the living room and basement. He positioned his bottles so he could sneak a drink while in any room in the house.

I was in elementary school when we were coming home from a Christmas family gathering in East Chicago. My inebriated father swerved the car back and forth, over the median line several times, and back to the shoulder of the road. My mother asked him to stay on the road, and though he slurred an incomprehensible response, she could tell he was irritated.

Shnicks and I were in the back seat and had dozed off from the long, eventful day. Suddenly a violent jerk woke us up as we slammed into the passenger's side of the car. My dad had fallen asleep, and my mom had quickly turned the wheel to veer the car away from a light post. My mom saved all our lives that night. But, somehow, this enraged my dad.

"Damn it, Helen! What the hell you doin'?" He pushed her off the wheel and swore he was in control of the car. "I'm fine. Don't be grabbin' the wheel. Hell, you 'bout to make me wreck the damn car and kill us all!" She grabbed the wheel from him on several occasions; she often assumed responsibility for things he didn't manage. She did her best to shield us from his destructive behavior, but often she was just no match for him.

Shnicks and I were about nine and ten years old when my dad woke us from our deep sleep one night. I couldn't quite understand what was happening. I could hear my mom pleading, "Don't wake them up, Ted. It's two o'clock in the morning." But he was adamant that we both come downstairs.

We wiped the dried, crusted sleep from our eyes, marching down the steps, hearts racing with equal parts fear and curiosity. As he ordered us both to sit on the couch, I could see right away that he was inebriated and upset.

"Who left this nail polish on the coffee table?" his words slurred.

Still in a fog, neither of us answered fast enough. He began to wave around a .375 revolver, shouting, "Answer me, dammit! Who left this shit on the table?!"

I had never seen a gun that close before. My palms began sweating and my heart pounded. Shnicks and I followed our normal routine of apologizing, though we really had no idea what we were apologizing for. We wanted to de-escalate the situation as quickly as possible, having learned from past incidents not to rock the boat by disagreeing with him. We knew to agree, to say yes, and to maintain eye contact. Anything else would risk throwing gasoline on the fire.

"Ted, please! Put that away! The kids didn't do nothin'!" my mom tearfully pleaded.

He continued, "Shut up Helen! I wanna know who did it!" We remained frozen, imploring him silently. After his incomprehensible tirade, he dismissed us. As we crept back upstairs to bed, he apologized and mumbled his "I love yous."

That night, like so many others, I followed Shnicks back to her room. As I laid down, my hands still clammy, my heart racing, and my underarms soaked, I fixated on the shiny revolver and wondered about the odds he would return with another concocted reason to be upset. Drifting off to sleep, I promised to wash away the event, to never speak about it again, to pretend like it never happened.

* * *

My dad's drinking continued to jeopardize our safety. One brutally hot summer day, my dad left Shnicks and me in the car while he went inside the Blue Room, his main hangout spot. We thought it would only be for a few minutes, as he had promised, and not like all the other times when the wait felt like a marathon.

We started off talking, then played a few silly games, and then eventually I began pestering her and pulling her ponytails. After a while, we realized how hot and hungry we were as the ninety-degree heat began to bake us, even with the windows down. We bravely discussed going inside to get my dad, but fear kept us sitting in the car. Sweating profusely after what felt like a few hours, we were convinced our dad had forgotten about us. With no further discussion, Shnicks flung open the door with tears in her eyes and marched to the entrance of the adults-only club.

Shnicks came right back out, and I anxiously waited to hear what transpired. Before she could reach the car, my dad stumbled out behind her. He didn't apologize, but it was the quietest ride we had ever taken. Shnicks later told me what some of the guys said when she walked in there.

"Ted, that's your baby girl? What the hell? You left your kids in the car? It's ninety degrees out there. Get your ass outta here!" his buddy Tree had exclaimed.

"Yeah, Ted. That ain't right man," one of the regulars said. "That's just not right."

I think he was embarrassed. The words of his friends meant my dad knew he was wrong for once. Although she was my big sister by only thirteen months, I sure admired Shnicks' courage that day and on many days to follow.

* * *

During our childhood—the most formative years in our lives—we witnessed so much. Too much. The wounds were deep. It would be decades before I was able to start the healing process and begin to grapple with the trauma and anger that stemmed from the actions and inactions of my dad.

By the time I was nearing the end of elementary school, I began to notice that my mom—who was passive by nature— began to stand up for herself, to stand her own ground. She was no longer willing to tolerate my dad's nonsense, violence, or manipulation.

I believe she became more courageous for me and my sister. Something had to give.

The instability in our home, coupled with the sheer fear of what our dad might do from one day to the next, became too much for my sister and me to bear. We were tired of living in fear, so Shnicks and I asked my grandmother if we could live with her instead of at home in the chaos.

"Y'all talkin' crazy. You know your mama would have a fit if y'all weren't livin' with her," she said, peering at us through her big, rimmed glasses. Although she didn't agree with us, I noticed the crease above her brow and the concern in her voice. "I'll talk to your mama about what's goin' on."

We didn't know it at the time, but my grandmother put pressure on my mom to make a change for us. I'm not sure whether it was a specific conversation or a final incident that convinced her, but she had had enough.

My mom finally divorced my dad in December 1983. Most kids are devastated when their parents get divorced. My sister and I were the opposite. I knew a divorce was a well-deserved and appropriate move for my mom, my sister, and me.

The reality of the divorce hit home when my uncle Bobby, my mother's youngest brother, sat me down on the front porch one day. "You're the man of the house now, Dez. You gotta be strong for your mother and sister."

The words were coming out of his mouth, but all I could focus on was the pit in my stomach. *The man of the house?* At eleven years old, this was my rite of passage—a race I was expected to start running with no real warmup. We walked into the house, with Uncle Bobby's hand on my shoulder. I had not wished for this, nor was I ready for the finality of my dad leaving my house and my family.

I walked upstairs to my room and cried. The chances of our new family life feeling secure were slim to none. I knew my relationship with my dad wouldn't change much; we never had any significant conversations that I remember—ever.

One night, less than a year after my talk with Uncle Bobby, Shnicks and I were asleep upstairs when suddenly we were awakened by a loud noise. We ran into my mother's room. It took just a few seconds for me to decide that I was to investigate and, if necessary, to protect.

"Dez, you can't go down there," my mom urged. "I'll call the police."

"Ma, we can't wait for them. I'm going downstairs. I'll be okay," I said with as much assurance as I could muster. Then I told them to lock the bedroom door behind me while I crept down the stairs with my baseball bat, which my sweaty palms made difficult to grip.

With each step I silently descended, I was a little further from boyhood. If it was my turn to protect my family, then I was going to put up a fight. I was no stranger to a fight. My heart almost leapt out of my chest as I took the last few steps, listening to see where the intruder might be. As I crept down the last step onto the first floor, sweat beading on my forehead, I kept reminding myself, *I am the man of the house.*

I peeked around one corner—nothing there. I crept into the kitchen. Everything was still intact. I took a deep breath and went charging into my living room. I was relieved and disappointed to find out that one of the blinds had fallen, causing a picture to fall and breaking its glass frame.

"Thank you," I said to no one in particular, breathing a sigh of relief. I was proud of myself, and so were my mom and sister. I stayed up the rest of the night counting my blessings and thinking of what I would do if there was a next time.

* * *

In a way, I felt proud to be able to take on the burden of being the man of the house. But I also knew I wasn't enough. My mom bore the brunt of the realities of being a single parent, especially after being previously very dependent on my dad.

When they were first married, she didn't even know how to drive. Once she had children, she stopped working and relied on my dad's unstable income. After about four years, the financial stress became insurmountable. She was forced to begin working again. She used public transportation in the freezing cold, rain, sleet, and snow, as well as the sweltering hot summer days. After their divorce, my mom learned to drive. But that didn't mean things got easier right away. Financially, we still struggled.

My mother began to take more overtime hours to cover the bills. She worked in customer service for the electric company. Fortunately, she eventually bought a car, but sometimes she slept on the couch at work so she could pick up extra shifts, which kept her away from our home for what felt like days at a time.

During my senior year of high school, my mother pulled one of those day-and-night shifts. I was sleeping early one morning when I received a random, jarring phone call. I stumbled out of my warm bed and grabbed the phone on the third ring.

"Hello?" I answered groggily.

"I think your mom has been in an accident," an unfamiliar voice said. "It looks bad."

My heartbeat was deafening in my ears as I threw on my clothes and raced out the door. My friend Rodney lived right around the corner from me and rushed me to the scene. I was overwhelmed. As we arrived, I knew there was no way she could have survived without the grace of God. Her car was wrapped around a pole, the airbags had deployed, and glass was everywhere.

"Where is she?!" I yelled to the first emergency responder I saw. "Ma! Ma!" I continued to yell into the early morning air.

A man approached me and said, "I'm the one who called you. They already took your mom to the hospital. You should meet her there."

Miraculously, my mother walked away with bruised ribs, a bruised sternum, and a broken wrist. She had to take a few weeks off work, but she also needed to recover from the pure exhaustion. She had sacrificed so much to ensure my sister and I had everything we needed; it was her time to take a rest.

I made a vow that my future kids would never have to experience anything remotely close to what Shnicks and I had endured. I learned what it felt like to experience uncertainty, disappointment, resentment, and anger because of my dad's addiction and instability. I only wanted to be dependable and trustworthy. My mother taught me that. And I grew up with neighborhood friends who lived by a certain code: *Your word is your bond. Period.* I have tried to live up to that ever since.

CHAPTER 4

THE GAMES WE PLAYED

———

"Man, check up!" I thrust the basketball with conviction in the direction of DeWayne.

"You crazy! It's my ball. Out on you!" DeWayne bounced the beaten-up leather ball a couple times on the concrete court and then jogged to the top of the three-point line.

Never one to back down, I retorted, "Stop cryin' and play ball. No blood, no foul." I followed him across the court and gave him a playful shove.

"Whatever. You just scared 'cuz I'm 'bout to whip you out here!" DeWayne came back at me.

"Let me see you do it!"

That kind of banter on the court was the typical love language displayed in our friendly but competitive neighborhood games. Staying outside, playing basketball and football, running relay races—you name it—became my escape from the craziness. The trash talking was as much a part of the game as dribbling, shooting, running, and passing.

Anyone I grew up with knew that the code in our neighborhood was about loyalty, mental toughness, and pride. On the court or in a neighborhood game, you played hard.

You didn't whine and complain, and you knew you had to earn respect.

During the summers when I was in elementary school, I would spend all day playing a variety of games and sports with friends. Most often playing for hours, then bolting home to slap together a bologna and cheese sandwich, then racing back down the street with sandwich in hand, swallowing between breaths and hoping to catch the next game to minimize my wait time.

I played a bit of organized youth basketball, but my fondest memories came from Little League baseball. Initially, I chose baseball because my friends and I could walk to practice, roughly a mile away, over the train tracks to the Ambridge-Mann Baseball Field. Walking meant I didn't have to worry about anyone coming to pick me up. At that time, my mom had not yet learned to drive, and my dad was too unreliable. I had been stranded at too many practices. The disappointment would be too much to bear, so I found a sport I could play that didn't require me to depend on anyone. Those long walks with my friends and the fierce competition and camaraderie at those practices made me forget about any challenges at home.

I turned out to be a pretty solid Little League player. We had a competitive team, the Westbrook Blue Devils, with talented players committed to showing up every day. The field was not always manicured, and so we often found rocks, glass, and divots on the field. But that didn't stop us from playing our little hearts out. One of my best buddies back then was Detrick, whom we called Deek. We were lucky to have his dad, Louis Eldridge, as our coach. Coach Eldridge's full-time job was delivering mail. He was a patient, mild-mannered guy whom we did not want to disappoint.

Playing on the baseball diamond taught me to analyze each play, weigh my options: swing, don't swing, bunt, slide, dive, steal home. So many decisions, each one impacting the next. It kept my mind busy and challenged me in a way that made me feel free. Slowly, I started to release some of my negative energy and emotions.

I'll never forget the one baseball game where my dad popped up. I was incredibly excited when I noticed him in my periphery. I wanted so badly to make him proud. I started emulating Chicago Cubs second baseman Ryne Sandberg, trying to make my batting stance wide like his and anticipating my launch to catch a flyball whenever possible.

This was my time to shine and to show my dad that I could really play. The timing couldn't have been better. There was a runner on first, and the ball was hit up the middle. I was just able to get my glove on the ball and simultaneously step on second base. One runner out! I planted hard and with all my strength fired to first. The ball reached our first baseman a half step before the runner for the double play to end the inning! But the first base umpire didn't see it that way.

"Safe!" the umpire yelled.

"That's bullshit! He was out!" my dad yelled.

The cadence of my dad's voice and his deliberate pacing let me know he had been drinking again. He stumbled onto the field in my defense and began to argue with the umpire.

"What the hell you lookin' at, man? You know he was out!"

He then started spewing insults. It took my coach and several other fathers in the stands to escort my dad off the field.

"Come on, Ted. Let the umpire call the game. You holdin' it up!" was the vague cry from other onlookers embarrassed by my father's actions but not moved enough to mitigate the scene he had caused.

I wanted to vanish from the field as my dad was escorted off. I completely lost my concentration. It is every kid's dream to have his father show up to games and watch him perform. My father *never* came. When he finally showed up, he showed out. He was a spectacle. Some of my teammates attempted to console me. Several gave me a pat on the back, and others said what they could to relieve some of the pain they knew I was experiencing.

As we walked from the field after the inning, Deek said, "It's okay, Dez. He was right, man. You got that guy out."

Another teammate, whose father was also dealing with alcoholism, tried to empathize with me, saying, "That's why I'm glad my dad doesn't come to the games, either." His words made me feel less lonely, less like something was wrong with me.

* * *

Many neighborhood friends became a part of my lifeline growing up. Their presence and participation in the alley kickball games, on the asphalt backyard basketball courts, in the basement floor hockey games all contributed to my ability to escape my challenges at home and tap into a world where I felt I belonged, one where I was more in control and where I could appreciate the consistency of the rules of the game.

Although most of our shenanigans would never make an ESPN highlight reel, I fondly remember some amazing athletic talent that gained the respect of the entire neighborhood. If the camera crews were available, they would have caught some intense games of tackle football on the "Sandlot." The Sandlot was the less-than-impressive field in front of Vohr Elementary School, which most of my buddies and I attended.

In fourth grade, I remember one such tackle football game that was down to the wire. I lined up next to Deek on the offensive line. There was no trophy to vie for, no championship title at stake. But our desire for bragging rights was just as intense.

The ball was hiked. Although my legs were tired and my belly had long informed me it was time to run home for a bologna and cheese sandwich, I bolted off the line and blocked my guy with all the strength I could muster. Deek sprinted forward, then darted diagonally in his post route. Although NFL star Odell Beckham Jr.'s claim to fame is his one-handed touchdown catch, Deek made the first one-handed catch I ever saw. When he stretched his right arm above his head as he leaped what seemed like ten feet in the air and grabbed the ball, we went absolutely bananas. Our team ran to pile on top of him in a blob of celebration, high-fiving, and laughing. Even our opponents cheered in amazement at Deek's legendary one-handed stick.

I lived for those games and competitions. Often, while in school, I would perk up as soon as I felt a light tap on my shoulder from a classmate who then handed me the crumpled piece of notebook paper that listed the teams for the lunchtime game. Our teachers never knew how, right under their noses, we orchestrated complex tournament brackets and balanced team rosters while we were supposed to be learning how to multiply fractions. Those days shaped our creativity, critical thinking, and athleticism.

Even so, without the resources of more affluent neighborhoods in Indiana, we used sticks for bats and buckets for bases. We used rags for flag football and sometimes broomsticks for hockey. We were still being fed hoop dreams from our community, along with other sports, as the only ambitions we could have in order to make it out of our city, which was dwindling economically. We thrived on imagining ourselves as superstar athletes and financially supporting our family and friends, but for so many of us, it was our only dream and, we thought, our only option.

These joint goals bonded us in a brotherhood, and we looked forward to those long summer days—the days we didn't have to worry about anything except having fun as kids. It was our outlet. And it was my life.

CHAPTER 5

A TALE OF TWO CITIES

—

Growing up as a kid in the 1970s and '80s in Gary, I didn't know much about the history of my hometown. As an adult, I realized that most people hadn't even heard of it and that those who had didn't think much of it. They might look at the dilapidated buildings, the Black folks hanging out on the streets, and the sighting of an old-timer in a purple or red suit and think the city didn't have much to offer.

What I knew about Gary was that I felt an incredible sense of pride and genuine connection to my community. As I walked toward my modest red brick, two-story house from school or to the park to play ball, it was customary for me to see neighbors and familiar faces who would eagerly greet me. A smile. A wave. Sometimes, a personal greeting.

"Hey, Dez! How's your mom doing?" or, "Be careful crossing Fifth Avenue, sweetie!"

After leaving our Westbrook apartment at age six, my neighborhood was a collection of other well-built, detached homes with spacious front yards and very few fences. That allowed us to run across several front lawns during neighborhood snowball fights and relay races.

The energy of the city is what I remember most. I could just be myself. Who I was as a person, as a Black person, was affirmed. I didn't feel the lack of resources or the oppressive systems at the time. I felt seen, accepted, and loved. Gary was home. Gary was me.

Gary was a planned city, developed in 1906. The US Steel Corporation was responsible for designing what is still the country's largest company town. It was appropriately coined "The Steel City" to reflect its founders' vision of creating a booming town on the backs of the steel industry. By the 1940s, Gary was a refuge for immigrants and Blacks from the South as a part of the Great Migration. Gary attracted all types of people seeking the American dream. (Davich, 2015)

By the time I was growing up, the promise of the city had dissipated. The steel mill industry was drying up, White flight left significant economic gaps, and opportunities in nearby Chicago lured many Black people to abandon my hometown. The Gary I grew up in was predictable. Either you perpetuated the cycle, or you risked ending up at the wrong place at the wrong time. Either way, you couldn't escape trouble.

Despite the many struggles, our city had a ton of character. And not just because the Jackson Five are from there.

I remember shopping at The Village on Grant Street. The commercial and retail district seemed so vibrant. I never liked shopping, but I loved seeing all the people. We always ran into someone we knew. While my mom and sister took their time in the grocery stores and clothing stores such as JCPenney, Montgomery Ward, and Sears, I found my own adventures playing hide and seek, driving my mom crazy.

One time, my shenanigans in the A&P grocery store resulted in me needing eight stitches in my forehead. That

Saturday morning, my mom, sister, and aunt seemed to take forever, moseying through every aisle and examining every label and price tag. By the time they had two full carts, I was deep into my game of darting down each aisle, weaving between carts and people as quickly as I could. As I turned the corner at the end of one aisle to race up the next, I ran smack into the aluminum wire edge of someone's cart. It stopped me cold. In a daze, I heard frantic shouts and wondered what the commotion was about.

When Aunt Shirley saw the blood and the gash, her nurse instincts kicked in. She immediately said to my mom, "Helen, we gotta get him to the hospital. He's going to need stitches."

Regardless of the bumps and bruises in our lives, we always looked out for one another. We felt as if we had everything we needed right there in Gary, with the stable support network of immediate and extended family close by. It wasn't a lot, but it was more than enough for me.

Even school started out as a safe haven. I was fortunate enough to start my elementary years in a gifted and talented math program. There is no doubt that this laid my foundation as a critical and analytical thinker.

I felt supported by teachers such as Ms. James, Ms. Hatten, and Ms. Graham. They were excited to teach me, and I could tell they believed in me. By the time I reached sixth grade and entered middle school, school was just a game. I learned how to squeak by and was no longer curious about learning.

One day, I was sitting in a middle school class with knots in my stomach. It seemed as if everyone else was able to read the chapters in our literature book and answer the questions much faster than me. I always had to go back and reread passages because I couldn't remember what I read. I began to dread most of my classes and, ultimately, school became boring.

I was often distracted with whatever was going on outside the window of my classrooms: birds, trucks, the rain. Sometimes I was distracted by thoughts of my family chaos. My dad came around, inconsistently, trying to win back my mother's heart. He didn't really show an interest in what I was up to, so his unexpected visits just created more turbulence for all of us.

"Pay attention, Desmond," my teachers would say, walking past my desk and tapping it to get me to refocus. The idea that I would one day write a book would have been laughable back then.

I didn't know it at the time, but one of the reasons school became harder was due to my undiagnosed dyslexia. As the passages got longer, it became more difficult to quickly and accurately process what I was reading. I would mix up the spelling of words, even ones I knew how to spell and had done so correctly before. I lost confidence and shied away from even attempting to read more complex texts, further inhibiting my development as I moved up in school.

In most of my classes, it didn't take much to get a passing grade, so I was compliant and did just enough not to fail. I went to school for recess and PE, where the games and competitions often resulted in tussles. I was quick to stand my ground, and frankly, my fuse was short. Typically, I was laid back and easy to get along with. But when tested, I would flip the switch, and my temper would flare. Even a minor misunderstanding at Tolleston Middle School quickly resulted in a full-blown yelling match, which escalated to shoving, and then a fury of punches.

One of these fights happened in seventh grade during Mr. Whiteside's math class. I was doing the practice problems on my worksheet when Lawrence walked by me and pushed my elbow, causing me to erroneously write across my paper. He snorted, showing his crooked smile. He was trying to be a funny guy, and it worked. The class started cracking up, and I was not happy about it.

I hopped up, exclaiming, "Man, you got the wrong one!" He continued to snicker and kept moving back to his seat. *Oh, he tryin' to make me look bad, huh?* I thought. *I'll show him I ain't no chump!*

I couldn't let it go and started after him. Before Mr. Whiteside could get up from his desk, I got close enough to Lawrence to give him a good, solid shove, causing him to stumble into his desk. The class cracked up again. Lawrence retaliated, and after a few blows from either side, Mr. Whiteside separated us, forcing us to cool off.

I thought that was the end of it, but later that afternoon, I was sitting in English class when I caught a glimpse of the back of a woman's head just outside of our open class door. The loose black and gray curls were strangely familiar.

Was that Mama Hattie? I immediately straightened my back and focused my eyes on the chalkboard. For those next few minutes, I was the most attentive kid in class, but that was cut short when I was called to the principal's office. My palms got sweatier as I walked down the hallway. I was not afraid of the principal and the suspension I knew was inevitable. I was terrified of the possibility of seeing Mama Hattie on the other side of the office door. Mr. Whiteside was a family friend, but I definitely had no idea he would call home so quickly.

When I got to the office, the secretary nodded toward the principal's inner door. As I slinked in, Mama Hattie sat in the chair in front of the principal's desk. The conversation was a blur. I nodded when I thought appropriate, but my mind raced ahead, trying to figure out how I could avoid riding home with Mama Hattie. I knew what her wrath could look and feel like, and I would rather be anywhere else but with her when she was upset.

"Boy what were you thinking!" she began once we got outside. "You got the school calling me 'cuz you keep actin' up, and they said your grades are bad!" She took a breath and started up again. "You know betta, Dez! You know your momma is workin' her butt off tryin' to make sure you and your sister are taken care of, and you up here actin' a fool at school! Shame on you!"

When we got in the car, she slammed the door and gave me a solid whack on the back of my head. My eyes teared up as I felt her disdain. I quickly but unsuccessfully tried to hold back the tears. The ride home was more of the same ranting, but I blocked most of it out as I focused on pushing down my feelings of rejection and unworthiness, hiding them from her and from everyone else.

I was used to just scraping along. I made it to high school, but barely.

Horace Mann High School opened in 1928, during a time when legal segregation still existed in the United States. Originally built for White students and named after a prominent proponent of public education in the United States, it had a beautiful landscape that featured a pond, rolling hills, a ravine, and a bird sanctuary. The school had a swimming pool and several gyms inside its massive Roman-inspired architecture. (Bullet, 2020)

By the time I was a student in the late 1980s, Horace Mann had evolved from an all-White school into an all-Black school. The landscape was lackluster, and we joked about how the grass from the old pictures had disappeared. Our field was not in good enough shape to host football games, and our swimming pool was empty and unusable.

Though we did have school spirit, often displayed in a sea of red and grey energy at sports games, our reality also included tension and violence. There was a fight or two almost every day. I'm ashamed to say that I was a part of a handful of them. As a teenager, I never hung out at a party or public social gathering that ended at its scheduled time. It was always cut prematurely by a fight or gunshots.

Despite the inherent adversity, I finally had a personal academic breakthrough in tenth grade. It was in Mr. Harvey's geometry class. He recognized I had a good memory and always complimented me on my analytical thinking. This was a huge confidence boost.

I would easily manipulate different formulas, theorems and postulates to figure out simpler ways to calculate the answer than the textbook. Mr. Harvey was pretty laid back, about average height with short, cropped salt-and-pepper hair. Often, he would hand over his chalk and take a seat.

"Go on, Desmond. Show the class how you solved it. I think your way is better than mine!" he would say affectionately, peering through his large, rimmed glasses.

This permission, this encouragement, this freedom from Mr. Harvey gave me agency and autonomy in the classroom. It was powerful. I felt validated standing at the chalkboard, eyes on me, as my teacher and my classmates looked at me. Those days in Mr. Harvey's class activated my creative and analytical capacities and, most of all, raised my confidence and self-esteem. I realized I did not have to be the version of myself rooted in the inadequacies I felt. I could rise to a truer version of myself.

In stark contrast during my senior year of high school, I had an English teacher named Mrs. Smith who challenged me and frankly would not give me any room to breathe. She didn't accept any late work, only allowed me one bathroom pass per semester, and wouldn't hesitate to let my mother or grandmother know when I was off track.

Mrs. Smith routinely changed our seating chart after every exam, arranging us based on our updated grade calculation. My best friend Byron and I would typically compete for the next-to-last chair. As long as we weren't last, we thought we had accomplished something. I actually had the audacity to laugh at him when he sat in the last seat, and I was only one seat ahead and 0.1 grade point average higher. I wonder why I didn't feel any shame or why I didn't question her practice. I just accepted I was supposed to be in that last row and often in that last chair. I didn't see myself as someone who was supposed to do well in school.

One day after class, Mrs. Smith asked me to stay for yet another conversation. "Dez, you know I've been on you all semester. You just aren't working hard enough in my class. The way you're performing right now, you and I will get reacquainted in summer school."

Her last comment resonated in a way that none of her others had before. My shoulders slumped, and I couldn't meet her gaze. I could feel her hope in me dissipating, needling a hole in my pride. She did not think I was capable. I needed to show her she was wrong. She could see I was capable if I just had someone to push me in the right direction with the right motivation.

Our next exam, Shakespeare's *Hamlet,* was three days later. I convinced Byron to join me in pulling all-night study sessions. Our goal was to avoid the last two seats once Mrs. Smith revealed the new seating chart. On the first night, we gathered snacks and hunkered in my basement. We memorized lines, we rewrote our notes, and we created flashcards. And when one of us fell asleep, the other gave a big shove to disrupt the nap we both longed for. We did everything we could to ensure we understood the vocabulary, the character development, and the plot.

I studied while I ate. I flipped through my flashcards while brushing my teeth. I needed to prove something to myself and to Mrs. Smith. In my mind, this exam was a competition, one I needed to win. I had faced big opponents on the court, on the field, in all those neighborhood games. I knew what it felt like to be the underdog.

By the second night of studying, I was a zombie, sleep-deprived but sleep avoidant. Byron and I quizzed each other, dozed off, woke each other, all while guzzling Mountain Dew.

On the morning of the exam, butterflies fluttered in my stomach. I kept reading my food-stained notecards as I walked to school and in my early morning classes. I couldn't calm the queasiness in my stomach as I walked into Mrs. Smith's class, but I had studied harder than I ever had before. It was a really good feeling to walk in knowing, for once, I was prepared.

I sat down and made sure I had an extra-sharp pencil. *Let's go, Son.* I put my head down and dug in. With each question, I grew more excited. I actually knew most of the answers! I was proud of being able to analyze the questions and confirm the answers based on studying. After a while, my concern about my place on the seating chart faded from my mind.

The next day, when Mrs. Smith announced the seating chart, Byron and I were numbers twenty and twenty-one out of thirty. We leaped over a handful of classmates and, best of all, moved out of the "F" row! But even more astounding, we had two of the highest grades on the test.

At the end of class, Mrs. Smith handed me an envelope dated two months prior. It was a note from her that said, "I knew you could do it, Dez."

I learned a valuable lesson. It was simple. I had worked hard at school; I had gotten results. Dyslexia or not, it was up to me to find a way to get the job done.

My high school days were filled with academic peaks and valleys. I had some good teachers, and some who never got to know me and my dreams.

I wish I could say that it was all the learning that made the best high school memories for me. But it wasn't. In fact, the experience was even further tarnished with Gary's despairing reality.

One evening, I went to a basketball game with Byron. The game was at Roosevelt High School, directly across the street from the Delaney community housing project and approximately two miles south of Horace Mann. After the game was over, I left and walked to my car. Before I put my key in the ignition, I looked up, and my jaw dropped. I saw two guys running with sheer fear on their faces and a mob of what looked like at least twenty people in hot pursuit. Quickly, I realized they were headed toward me. My heart raced as I fumbled with my keys. The two poor souls passed me and scrambled into the car next to mine. Unfortunately, they didn't have enough time to start the car and drive off. The mob caught them, and what I witnessed next would haunt me for years. It was one of the most unfair fights I had ever seen.

Several guys from the mob jumped on top of the hood. Others smashed the windows. Eventually the two guys who tried to find safety in the car were dragged onto the pavement. And that's when the stomping and kicking began with ferocious intensity. The screams and the moans sickened me. And then they stopped.

The car in front of me looked as if it had gone through a compactor. The two guys lay still and silent.

One of the gang members looked at my license plate and yelled through my rolled-up windows, "We know where to find you!" Code for: *We have no issues with you as long as you mind your business.* The mob ran off in celebratory fashion.

After I gathered myself, I sped out of the parking lot with my mind fixated on those two boys. These types of mob fights and gang activity were rampant. The Disciples, Vice Lords, and neighborhood cliques were just a few of the gangs, along with other territorial crews and clans from various projects. I didn't realize until I was much older just how unhealthy this environment was. It was just normal for me to see fights and violence and despair.

In my case, I kept my head down and focused on sports, especially when my academics were struggling. I lived for the competition and camaraderie that sports provided. I didn't go looking for trouble, and I was lucky it didn't come find me. I saw the older guys who were serious athletes, and they were given an "athlete's pass," which meant the active gang members would steer clear. It meant you got to travel through the hood and avoid harassment. It was as if vagrants and gang members acknowledged that athletes had a chance to be successful and rallied around them.

Athlete or not, there were still dangerous and senseless rites of passage we encountered in Gary, such as "knockout." It was a game in which guys would bet on each other to blind-side punch a stranger, and each guy would have one punch to knock someone out. I know for most people this game seems outrageous. I often remind my students, my cohorts, and my peers that when a person is not properly educated from early childhood, their opportunities for success become more and more narrow. As a result, this same person at some point has no vision for their future and, most of all, no hope. This is a dangerous state of mind to be in. You are angry, hypervigilant. You don't have hope or respect for yourself, and therefore you have absolutely zero respect for others, meaning you have no problem punching and hurting a random person.

The hope and trauma of Gary were instrumental in shaping my identity. The support from my family and friends sustained me. At the same time, the lack of resources in the city limited my opportunities. As deeply as I felt connected to Gary, I also felt compelled to see what other places and opportunities could offer me.

CHAPTER 6

PUSHING THE LIMITS

—

Back in the summer before I started high school, I lived at the basketball courts. My hoop dreams were a vivid part of my imagination. It felt like my path forward.

One hot summer day in August, about two weeks before classes started for my freshman year, I was out shooting ball with a few friends. We had been outside for a few hours, but we were far from calling it a day.

"Hey y'all, I'm out," said one of the taller guys I didn't know very well.

"Naw, man, come on. If you leave, then the teams will be uneven," I responded.

"I gotta get home, take a break, then head over to Mann for cross country practice," he offered as he kept walking off the court.

The dreadful memories from my tryout in seventh grade came rushing back. I said adamantly, "Oh, heck no! I'm not doing that again. I'm going out for the basketball team in the winter and maybe baseball in the spring."

I was caught off guard when he replied with a shrug, "All basketball players have to play football or run cross country."

I was floored! *Were the middle and high school basketball coaches related!?* There had to be some conspiracy.

Two hours later, I trudged to cross country practice. I didn't know that decision would change the trajectory of my life. Exhausted from playing in the sun, I was discouraged and unprepared to endure another laboring tryout. But I set my mind on my ultimate goal. I loved basketball, and more than anything, I wanted to make the freshman team. I quickly identified the tall, burly man who controlled the clipboard and the whistle. I met *the* coach, Roosevelt Pulliam. Everyone called him "Chief." He was a leader who commanded respect with his mere presence. Although the word chief has unfortunately been used as a microaggression to indigenous people and First Nations, we referred to Coach Pulliam as "Chief" because we had the highest regard for him.

As I walked up to introduce myself, Chief quickly grunted, "It's too late to come out, son. The first meet is only a few weeks away. You won't have time to get ready, but if you really want to give it a shot today, I won't stop you." His smirk made me realize that he didn't think I stood a chance.

We were all transported to our practice course about three and a half miles south of Mann.

Chief partnered me with Wyman Ashford, a junior who was a veteran on the team.

Chief said, "If you keep up today, I'll invite you back." *At least this time I knew not to race to the front and burn out before I could finish.*

My previous experience trying out in middle school gave me warning about how this would feel. Even though I was not looking forward to the run, I knew I could hang in there.

Once Chief walked away, Wyman said, "Hey, man, what's your name?"

I looked at him, noticing that he was stocky and muscular, more of a football build than a distance runner. I replied, "Desmond, but everyone calls me Dez. I'm gonna be a freshman when classes start."

"I can tell," he chuckled and smiled. "Just try and stick with me. I won't kill you today. I'll keep the pace nice and easy this time. Don't worry. You'll be fine."

Wyman and I began to trot away in smoldering heat at the apex of the sun's intensity. It was hot, humid, and miserable. Oh, and I had on basketball shoes. At some point during the first portion of the run, Chief's words resonated in my head, *If you keep up today, I'll invite you back.* I had only one shot.

I swallowed what little saliva I had in my mouth, which was becoming more and more dry. Almost two miles in, it became harder and harder to breathe. Wyman tried to keep a good conversation going, asking a ton of questions, but eventually I couldn't muster the oxygen and strength to answer. I was conserving every breath, trying to pull and use every molecule of air left in my lungs. Over and over, my mind pleaded, *When will this be over? When will this be over?*

Finally, Wyman said, "We're almost there, man." My worries were allayed. But "almost there," much to my chagrin, was not the end. It was only our turnaround point, still one mile away. My face frowned in disbelief. I kept pushing forward, my chest tightened, and my pulse pounded in my ears. *Only halfway there?* My legs threatened to give out with each step. *How am I going to find the strength to keep going?*

I needed a reason to stop. I thought quickly then knelt down to untie my shoe, only to tie it back again, giving myself a chance to regroup and catch my breath. There was a split second when I considered giving up, but my mind quickly raced back to how I felt when I was cut from my seventh-grade cross country team. Not making the high school basketball team as a result of being cut from cross country was not an option. I only weighed 128 pounds, so football was not going to happen. In the milliseconds it took me to weigh my options, I realized I was in it until the finish. *Come on, Dez. You got this!* I pulled myself up and continued on.

But then, within my weakened state, I began to replay my past in my mind—how unworthy my dad made me feel, how my mother made sacrifices on a daily basis.

Replaying what I had heard too often—*Dez, you're too small, you're too slow, and you don't have the talent!*—made me dig deeper to stay committed to the pace Wyman set. *Come on Dez. You can do this!* I was feeling something I had never felt before, but it wasn't about the pain. I craved the reward. I desperately wanted to make a school team for the first time. I wanted to feel proud and wanted and worthy. I wanted to feel as if I belonged. And I wanted to carve out a space of my own. Somewhere deep down, I felt running was going to help me make my mark in the world.

Struggling to breathe, I felt my cardio go first. Then the cramping began, followed by a complete buildup of lactic acid in my legs. Body blow after body blow, I was in for the grind. I kept mumbling to myself: *Come on, Dez, just hang on.* Right at the moment when I nearly lost all confidence that I would ever be able to breathe normally again, Wyman released those sweet words again: "We're almost there."

We were close to the golf course at Gleason Park when he panted, "If you can keep a secret, we can dip into that clubhouse to get a sip of water."

I immediately gasped, "I won't say a word!"

"One more thing," he offered. "You have to hurry and get a couple of sips before they kick us out!"

"Deal!" I responded acceptingly.

We entered the air-conditioned golf clubhouse, sweating profusely, and noticed right away that many of the golfers were not happy that we bombarded their clubhouse. Wyman kept his word and took a mere second and a half to take a couple of sips. But my body betrayed me and Wyman as I took five, six, maybe seven seconds worth of sips, just long enough for the Gleason Park manager to notice us and then yell at us to get out. It was the best water I ever tasted. That water gave me the fuel to get back to the run with stoicism.

We hit the door, and Wyman began to run. I followed his lead, and right away I was back in pain. That familiar feeling in my chest made me more anxious with each step. The burning in my chest, the restriction in my airways, the weakness in my limbs were all the preliminary signs to a much-dreaded asthma attack. *Should I stop? Did I bring my inhaler?* I just couldn't risk it.

I could not bring myself to run any faster. I was sandbagging the run to a pedestrian pace. The closer we got, the more encouraging Wyman became. Although sweat poured down his face and his T-shirt was drenched, Wyman didn't look as if he was in pain. "Come on, Dez. You got this, man!" he encouraged me. "You want to make the team? Keep going. Just don't stop!"

Eventually, I spotted the finish line with about 800 meters left. My eyes fixated on where I wanted to be rather than how little air my lungs allowed into my body.

Quite a few of the guys had finished already and began to cheer us on. Anthony Williams, a sophomore with a short Jheri curl and sideways grin, met us with 600 meters to go as he realized I was struggling and ran the rest of the way with us. He told me to relax, lift my knees, and pump my arms. Somehow, I survived. I made it. And then, I collapsed.

I lay on the ground with a masochistic grin, even though I was in sheer pain.

"Nice job, Desmond 'Tutu,'" Chief teased. We'll see you tomorrow."

I had made the team. I felt an overwhelming sense of gratification and accomplishment.

My relationship with running officially began that day. I had never experienced this type of satisfaction from any other sport. It was settled. I was all in, and I fell hard and fast. I learned more about myself in my first week of cross country practice than I had in all the years of playing other sports. I loved the camaraderie, but I also loved challenging myself to extend and push mentally and physically.

In the following weeks, I would get to know the rest of the guys on the team. They were great athletes but better people. These guys showed up every day, committed to one another and focused on a common goal. They had a level of pride and dedication I had never seen before.

The team made a community possible. The men on that team inspired me. I carry their stories with me into coaching.

Anthony Williams was our top runner. In 1988, he became the first Black high school student-athlete to win a 5,000-meter state championship in cross country in the United States. He even received a congratulatory letter from former president Ronald Reagan.

Our team was then blessed to have Eric Smoot join us, and boy was he resilient. Despite his talent and his eventual entry into the Indiana Hall of Fame for his championship titles, Smoot's challenging home situation lessened the sting of my own.

Eric was unhoused. Both of his parents were addicted to drugs, so he found solace where he could. At times it was at his older siblings' homes. Other times, it was at his teammates' homes. He hopped around for a while until he and our teammate Jeff Finch became best friends. Eventually Jeff's family opened their door to Eric, and he lived with them for the rest of his high school years. Our team became Eric's family. It was his outlet, and it saved his life. Anthony and Eric set the tone and paved the way for the culture of our program. They were the gold standard, and everyone, including me, wanted to follow their footsteps.

This unique community of teammates laid the foundation for my life ahead, revealing the example I would attempt to emulate with every team I coached.

CHAPTER 7

HAIL TO THE CHIEF

———

Running demanded so much of me—mentally, physically, and emotionally. It fostered my grit while defining my perspective and character.

I was consumed even when I wasn't running. It was the personal sacrifices, the cramps, the lightheadedness, the stomach pains, even feeling like my legs were as heavy as a sack of potatoes. The sheer pain let me know I was still in the game during the last mile of a practice or a race. Somehow, these challenges became my reward. My teammates relied on me for motivation, and I could count on them, too. This brotherhood fueled the intensity with which I approached each practice and each meet.

However, it was the love and leadership of my coach, Chief, that provided the supportive foundation for me to not only compete, but to excel. He quickly became one of the most influential figures and forces in my formative years and throughout my life.

Chief was a big burly guy with a thick black Jheri curl, standing about six feet, three inches tall. He demanded the best from everyone. He would say, "Champions and successful people get comfortable being uncomfortable." His dark brown skin was deeply sunbaked from all the hours he spent outside training the team during the cross country preseason in the summer. If we did not give Chief our best, there would be consequences. We got used to the extra sprints at the end of practice, another set of push-ups when our arms already felt like spaghetti, or those killer repeat 800-meter runs if we didn't give our best effort.

By no means was he light on us, but the entire team always wanted to live up to his standards and expectations out of sheer respect and trust. He was from the school of hard knocks and did not respect slackers or shortcuts. I inherited this trait from Chief. He was the first person in my life, besides my mom, who demanded this standard of high expectations and accountability on a daily basis. He showed up for me, so I would show up for him. I responded to this type of accountability. It worked then, it worked in Mrs. Smith's class, and it would continue to work in my life.

Chief articulated that running and life are all about how much you are willing to sacrifice and how hard you're willing to work. He would often say in that distinctive, gruff voice of his, "Hell, what you put in is what you get out!" This cause-and-effect relationship he so often referenced is something any distance runner or goal-oriented person can identify with. We sacrificed time hanging out with our other friends. We missed parties and dances. If any of us did have a girl we were inter-ested in, we didn't have time to date. We learned real success is not possible without discomfort or sacrifice.

After some time, we learned that beneath Chief's bark, he had the softest heart. Although we all called him Chief, he actually acquired that moniker because he referred to his runners as "chief" on a regular basis. He considered us leaders—a chief is a leader respected by his tribe. The nickname carried the power to remind us of how we should carry ourselves.

Chief was born Roosevelt Pulliam. For so many of us, he was the father figure we so desperately needed. He commanded respect in everything he did. When he spoke, we listened. He connected with each of us and made sure we felt seen.

Chief's upbringing was challenging, but he made no excuses. Decades after coaching me, I was grateful that Chief shared more about his life with me. It made me appreciate him even more. He learned at a young age that he needed to take advantage of any resources and opportunities available to him. He was the son of a sharecropper in Westpoint, Mississippi. He never met his dad. He was the youngest of nine siblings. He recalled being strapped to his mother's back as she traveled and worked in the desperate and suffocating heat of the Delta. Unfortunately, Chief lost his mother in a car accident when he was only four years old.

Chief's childhood experiences drove him to do everything he could to make sure none of his own students or athletes felt "less than." He would often buy us breakfast, lunch, training shoes, and school supplies. He even lured some talented runners in with his free meal antics. He was the antithesis of the teacher who shamed him and his classmates.

My teammates and I knew if we were committed to working hard, we could count on Chief for absolutely anything.

Chief wanted his team to have a killer instinct on and off the track. Back then, Horace Mann High School had no track and often practiced on a street adjacent to the school. Chief would block off the street using construction cones.

Many residents viewed this as an inconvenience. However, once they realized it was for teenage boys to work out and be a part of something positive and special, they applauded Chief's efforts. Of course, there were complaints from time to time, but these were far outweighed by the support he garnered from the neighborhood and from the school.

Still, we would periodically hear someone laying on their car horn suggesting that Chief needed to move the cones affecting the flow of traffic immediately. Every so often, a disgruntled driver would get out of their car to question Chief's motives. First, the closer they got to Chief, the more they noticed Chief's stature and stoic look. Second, they would quickly realize that Chief didn't want friction; he would approach them with his arms outstretched and plead his case.

"Look, I'm sorry, but we have no track. It's full of gravel, rocks, glass, and Lord knows what else. Can you please bear with us? These kids are dedicated to something positive, and if they don't have this opportunity, some of them will be on the streets." Chief always had his way with words, and most people he encountered could sense his passion for us, defusing the situation quickly.

Chief's philosophy with running and life were parallel: trust hard work and dedication, take pride in all you do, accept no handouts, and be the best at whatever you do. Sometimes those lessons were learned the hard way.

It was winter break during my junior year, and I was startled out of sleep by the blaring of my alarm clock.

"Uuuugh," I moaned, slapping my hand across my nightstand behind me in an effort to find and silence the source of the unwelcomed noise. This was supposed to be a relaxing and fun winter school break—two weeks of late-night snacks and movie watching followed by sleeping in until noon.

I managed just enough energy to roll my body over to turn off my alarm clock and almost fell out of bed. *Darn it!* I had forgotten that I moved the clock across the room to force myself to get up. I felt like I was sleepwalking. I stumbled to the bathroom to splash cold water on my face and took somebody's wash rag to get the sleep out of my eyes. Like most of my teammates, I was upset and annoyed that we had a 6:30 a.m. practice every weekday during our break. I plodded through downstairs and into the kitchen to toss two pieces of wheat bread into the toaster. I put a dab of jelly on my toast to give me a tiny jolt of sugar and flavor. In three quick bites, I devoured each piece and prepared to face the elements.

As I layered up and stepped out into the blistering December cold, I was met with a biting wind that felt like tiny needles on my face. My hands trembled as I attempted to lock the door. I shook my head, hopped down my porch step in one leap, and ran the three short blocks to the school under the blue and orange dawn of the day.

"Alright, guys. The plan is to run outside and warm up in between your repeat intervals inside. Let's make this workout short and sweet. Since it's only twenty-three degrees outside, you can finish your mileage inside and in the hallways after your five 800-meter repeats," Chief said, listing the key components of our workout for the day.

"Here are some extra socks to put on your hands and Vaseline to rub on your face and neck," he continued as he pointed at the clear bin of items on the ground next to him.

No one said a word. No one joked. We slowly got up, dragging our feet and hanging our heads as we prepared to cringe when the door opened to the bitter cold and the eager wind met us face-to-face again.

We started running the first part of our workout on the rugged gravel track, but we didn't put much effort into it. We didn't want to be at practice, and it showed.

"Damn it, guys, hit the times! If we're gonna be out here, let's get something out of it!" Chief shouted.

We barely responded, maybe picking up the pace just slightly, but we largely continued our lackadaisical effort.

"Hell, you guys aren't going to waste my time," Chief said after the third 800-meter interval. "Take your asses in the gym and have a seat in the bleachers!" he instructed.

We all filed in, trudging our way over to the bleachers, breathing heavily and sheepishly glancing at one another. We knew we had sandbagged the workout. As if abiding by an unspoken rule, we all attempted to sit on the back rows of the bleachers to avoid contact with our obviously disappointed coach.

Chief charged in behind us with a fire in his step. Pacing back and forth, he gave himself at least a ten-second countdown to cool down before he addressed us.

"Hell, guys, why are we here? Damn it, why are we here?! You're wasting my time, and most of all, you're wasting your own time. Time is valuable. It's something you can never get back. You're preparing for a cruel world, and absolutely nothing will be given to you." He paused his pacing and looked at us directly, hands crossed across his chest.

After about six seconds, he continued pacing and chastising. "You have to learn to be uncomfortable and not allow anything, and I mean anything, to stand in your way. It's one thing to have a goal, but it's another ballgame being Black and having a goal! You need to be ten times as thorough in everything you do just to get half as much. So, if you are going to be soft and whine and complain, find another team! I love you guys, but I would be doing a disservice to you all if I didn't tell you the harsh truth. Learn to give your best at everything you do and especially the things you don't necessarily like to do, and you will be successful in life!"

Chief knew that as Black men, we would face discrimination and inequities. Like so many in his generation, he reminded me and my teammates often of the disadvantages we faced and how important it was to know that even though life would never be fair for us, we still needed to strive for excellence if we wanted to experience success. When we traveled to meets in suburban areas outside of Gary, we were smacked head-on with our reality. The resources at those mostly White high schools were a stark reminder of what we didn't have.

But what we did have was who we felt was the best coach in the country, even when he did make us run outside in the dead winter. Chief actually only ran track and field up through middle school, but he was one of those adults who would have been great coaching anything because he understood people. The principles he taught us on the course and the track made us better men, helped us win in life.

With that instinct, Chief made me realize I'm only as successful as the seeds I plant in others. We often celebrate winning championships and personal records, and while I love them, the billion-dollar questions become: *Did my student-athletes grow as people under my care? Did they become better people or more prepared for life in general?* I derived these reflective questions from the example Chief set for me when I was a teenager. These seeds sprouted into a realization that leadership, commitment, and hard work make the difference between teams that win and teams that don't.

CHAPTER 8

WORTH MORE
THAN A RIBBON

Although distance running in a predominantly Black city was not initially popular when I was in high school, our team quickly garnered tremendous respect from our school, our community, and our city. It took many two-a-day runs during the summer and lots of socks on our hands in the blistering cold during the icy winters, but we were locked in and wanted to run our best as a team.

In most cross country meets our team attended in Indiana, the winners sat in lavish chairs in front of hundreds, sometimes thousands, of runners, spectators, and coaches during the awards presentations. Before the start of every race, I envisioned sitting in one of them. During my junior year, I knew I had a chance to place in the top ten at the Lafayette Jeff Invitational and take a seat among the esteemed finishers. I worked my butt off for the opportunity.

On that gray, fall day at the Lafayette course, we toed the starting line. The course was crisp, green, and surrounded by lush trees. The atmosphere was serene. I truly believe one of the most beautiful moments in a cross country race is the dead silence just before the gun goes off, when time seems to slow. You can feel the intensity of each athlete's focus, ready to go to war with their respective teammates, battling both their competitors and the clock.

Bang! went the starting gun. I sprinted out, my legs driven by my medaling intentions, and I situated myself in the top twenty. All was comfortable through the first 800 meters of the 5K race. *Get a rhythm, Dez,* I told myself. I settled into a rhythmic exchange between my breathing, my arms, and my legs. I was confidently in that zone, where my entire body felt free and in sync.

I hit the one-mile mark and strongly held my position. *That's it. Stay right here.* I was exactly where I wanted to be, tucked in the front pack. Half a minute later, my legs began to tire more than normal, so I attempted to relax to keep the acidity from taking over my entire lower body. Then my chest began to tighten. I realized my breathing was starting to labor. Feeling the familiar burn in my lungs made me want to panic. *It's too soon! Oh, God. There's too much of the course left!*

I hit the halfway point and slipped back to thirty-fifth place. My difficulties cascaded from that point on, my pride simultaneously taking a beating. I was not prepared to compete with the top pack. There would be no fancy chairs for me. Runners were easily striding past me. I crossed the finish line in a disappointing seventy-fifth place out of the field of nearly 300 runners. After the cooldown and ceremony, I felt completely defeated. I was given a seventy-fifth-place ribbon in the chute at the finish line.

As we were walking back to the bus, my head hung down and my feet dragged. I threw the ribbon down in a mud puddle and kept walking. I didn't realize Chief was nearby and witnessed my outburst.

"Desmond, pick up that ribbon! You ran like crap, so you can't be mad at anybody but yourself!"

Chief's booming voice felt like a slap on my face. I knew he was disappointed in my performance and my attitude. He went on to add salt to the wound: "You got what you deserved today. No one will ever give you anything worth having in life. You have to learn to prepare and go out there and take it."

I said nothing in response. No one challenged Chief. He was a giant to us, and we respected the hell out of him. As I sat on the bus for the hour ride home, I felt alone. I leaned my head back on the seat with my eyes closed. I was nauseous, and my head felt hollow. It was as if I didn't have a friend in the world. It's amazing how these kinds of feelings can become our reality, can shape who we are or who we become. My disposition made me unapproachable to my teammates.

About halfway through the drive home, Chief called me to the front of the bus and sat me down in the seat across from him. His comments were brief and direct: "Desmond, you're a nice guy, but you gotta get tough. You have a decision to make here. You will either keep feeling sorry for yourself and make excuses or you step up with your training and commitment!"

Reflecting more as I went back to my seat, I was disappointed in myself. I was angry that Chief didn't show any sympathy. I was afraid my teammates would not believe in me anymore.

Once we arrived back at our school, I got off the bus and started the three-block walk home. One of my teammates, Jeff, put his hand on my shoulder and said, "Don't forget we're family, man." Somehow, that statement and that positive energy lifted a weight off me. No feeling sorry for myself. I had more in me, and it was time to raise my efforts to meet my dreams.

I was a part of a special program with special teammates and no doubt a special coach. Going through the motions and showing up for every practice was not good enough. I had to set a daily goal, enjoy working hard toward it, and embrace the process along the way. I needed to start asking myself, *What did I do today to get one step closer to my goals?* I took the seventy-fifth-place ribbon and taped it next to my bedroom light switch. At times, it made me sick to look at. But it also reminded me of the feeling I never wanted to experience again. It motivated me to perform extra push-ups, core exercises, morning runs, and anything else that could prevent that scenario from unfolding again.

This adversity became the springboard to digging deeper. Up to that point, I thought I worked hard. But working hard fooled me into believing I couldn't work any harder.

* * *

By spring of my junior year, I was done licking my wounds and had leveled up my work ethic and commitment to the team. I had completely bought into Chief as my coach and mentor.

Chief picked a bold strategy at the state championship track meet that year. Anthony Williams was a senior and a role model for all of us younger guys on the team. He was the reigning Indiana cross country state champion. At the state meet, Anthony was instructed by Chief to run in lane two the entire way in the 1600 meters.

Chief gave these instructions to Anthony: "You will have to run your best race today and protect Smoot. Allow him to have the inside rail of lane one so he runs the shortest distance, and you control the pace. Don't let anyone pass you, and make sure Smoot does the least amount of work."

Chief's strategy to allow Smoot to run the least amount of distance increased his chances of running faster than the other runners who had to run in the outside lanes—lanes with a larger circumference. Chief knew Anthony was the fastest on the field and could afford to give Smoot the advantage of the inside lane. This way, they had the potential to finish first and second, scoring the maximum points in that race.

As he held off the rest of the field, Anthony used up so much of his energy that he was unable to stay ahead of his final competitor in the race—his teammate. Smoot mustered the energy to nip Anthony at the finish line in a photo finish. With Anthony's competitive spirit, he was disappointed with the runner-up position but at the same time ecstatic for Smoot and the eighteen points we garnered as a team for the one-two finish. He had been the ultimate team player. He executed the strategy perfectly and didn't neglect his responsibility to his team. It is a coach's dream when you have athletes who care more about their team's success than they do their individual success. This kind of commitment to running and to the team propelled Anthony to a successful running career at Kansas State University.

Chief cultivated this willingness to sacrifice for the team by being that type of role model. He demanded so much from us, but he trained us to demand as much from ourselves and from one another even in the most extreme conditions.

Training during the summer months was grueling. But I'd grown used to Chief pushing us beyond what we thought was possible. And the summer before my senior year was brutal.

During one practice, we embarked on a six-mile run from our high school to Gleason South Golf Course. After arriving at the golf course, we grabbed water and began stretching. Then Chief ordered us to meet him at West Side High School, about seven miles away. No big deal. We were used to six-mile "frolics," as Chief would call them, so seven miles seemed more than reasonable.

Many of us made light of the run, but glycogen depletion was becoming more of a factor with a couple of miles to go. Our mouths became dry, light-headedness set in, and our legs began to feel wobbly. Finally, Chief greeted us at West Side. We grabbed our sports drinks out of the big orange cooler again and had a light snack Chief offered us.

Before we could get too comfortable, Chief said, "Okay, in five minutes, meet me at Bowman Square."

It just got real. Bowman Square was four and a half miles away. We didn't complain; we just made the mental commitment, and the physical task followed. Once we reached Bowman Square, breathing hard, sweat pouring down our faces and backs, and we felt more than accomplished. I rested with my hands on my knees, still trying to regain composure in my breathing.

"Alright, cool down back to Mann," Chief ordered. "Add the long loop," he added, referring to an additional route that would make our entire workout a total of more than twenty miles for this Saturday morning.

"Man, that was crazy," I said to Eric, shaking my head as we stretched on the grass after practice.

"Chief must have lost his mind today," Eric replied. I nodded in agreement, thinking there would be no way I could pull myself up from the ground to walk home.

Years later, my teammates and I still debated whether this workout was more insane than the workout when we ran twenty-five 800-meter repeats. We thought Chief had lost his mind at times, but we later learned that it wasn't all about the physical work; he wanted us to always believe we could do the unthinkable. It worked. Many of us knew we could handle life as a result of Chief pushing us to our ultimate limits. He would always say, "Life will not be fair, so you have to prepare for whatever storm comes your way."

During my senior year, we finally had our chance to be one of the top cross country and distance programs in the state of Indiana. We had a chip on our shoulder because we had been pummeled by the suburban teams since my freshman year. I had upped my game big time, and now I had one last season to prove what I was made of, to showcase my hard work, my heart, and my grit.

At the second meet of the year, I realized that I was up for the painful challenge of breaking seventeen minutes on a standard 3.1-mile cross country course—a feat that only the top high school cross country runners could accomplish. I knew exactly where this battle had to be won. It needed to happen as I transitioned from mile two and into mile three. I was going to have to commit to the pace and believe in my training. I knew exactly what I was going to have to endure and welcomed the suffering.

That day was only a triangular meet versus city teams Gary Wirt High School and Lew Wallace High School, but it meant much more than a small-time meet for me. I had something to prove, and this was the day I was unwilling to allow the clock to strike seventeen minutes with me still on the course. As I came to the final mile, I began to feel heavy and had a burn in my quads while my labored breathing began to take over. I began telling myself, *Come on, Dez, you got this. Don't panic, keep your cool, take three deep breaths, and stay under control. Don't look for the finish line. Focus on form and cadence, and it will find you.*

I was feeling the discomfort and the agony down the home stretch with 800 meters to go. I knew I would approach this moment where my body would scream mercy, and on this day and in this moment, I was prepared to embrace the physical discomfort. I was committed to my cadence, and I was prepared to hit the override button, bullying my body to put one step in front of the other while maintaining my rhythm. That voice in my head again said, *Pain is temporary. Pride is forever. If you give up, you will never forgive yourself, and that pain will live forever.* The finish line was near. . . .

"16:45, 46, 47, 48," called my younger junior varsity teammates near the finish line.

"...16:50, 51, 52!" they yelled as I crossed the line.

I did it!

I pumped my fists in the air with a huge grin on my face as I staggered, legs wobbling precariously for a few paces after the finish line. I ignored the burning in my chest and the sweat pouring into my eyes to give my teammates high-fives and fist bumps. Finally, I had broken that seventeen-minute barrier. To provide some context, I had been stuck at my 17:24 personal record the year before. I came to embrace, even welcomed, putting my body through these laborious efforts again and again, knowing the results would make it all worth it. Chief taught us to elevate our minds beyond the pain. He always said, "You never reach your full potential until you learn to embrace discomfort and challenge." This was one of the greatest lessons in my life.

In the post season, we qualified to advance from sectionals to regionals. We won our third consecutive sectional title that year, and then it was time for the big boys: the regional championships. Regionals featured suburban powerhouse teams from Northwest Indiana and many of the top distance runners in the state. Jason Casiano, Jim Arnold, and Jeff Smenyak were among the cross country household names we aimed to beat.

There was no way I was going to let my team down at regionals. It was late fall 1989 at that point, and the autumn colors were fading into the bleakness of the inevitable winter. Once the race started, I was locked in and knew which pack I needed to be a part of, which runners I needed to separate from, and which hills I had to grind through. I gradually accelerated, and I never looked back. Even more exciting, I thought I was passing Valparaiso High School's fourth guy as I entered the chute at the end of the race, but I later learned I beat their third guy that day.

The rest of the team also stepped up, and it was the beginning of our team's journey to making history. We had grown used to the looks and stares and glares when we showed up at meets. We knew that expectations others had of us were pretty low. It was not common for an all-Black team to compete at high levels in cross country in Indiana at that time. We went on to take third at the regional championships and then had another strong showing in a steeper semi-state championship meet, finishing third again. We became the first African American team and first team from Gary to qualify for the 5K distance at the Indiana State Cross Country Championship Meet at Southgrove Golf Course in

Indianapolis. We competed respectfully at the state championships, but my performance was subpar, because I suffered a stress fracture in my foot at the qualifying meet a week earlier. I hobbled through the state championship race and finished a few steps ahead of the last place finisher.

My state finish wasn't ideal, but it couldn't dampen my overall experience with my teammates. I ran with some incredible guys. We had a crew of guys who ran sub-seventeen minutes: me; Harvey Bolds, with bad knees and all; Chester Washington and Anthony Bland, basketball superstars; Ricky Mitchell, a freshman phenom; Jeff Finch, known for his passion and motivational speeches; and Michael "Mad Dog" Johnson. In our area, being a sub-seventeen-minute cross country guy in high school earned you street cred in the sport. It is an achievement I still feel proud to tout.

Our hard work paid off. With commitment and dedication, dreams can come true for me and for anyone else. Some learn this grind at home; others learn it in school. I learned it on the course. Facing my failures and limitations taught me how to rebound and persevere.

That infamous seventy-fifth-place ribbon taped next to my light switch was a constant reminder of what I could do. It kept me hungry and humble, honing the fortitude I needed to propel my steps forward.

PART II

COLLEGE YEARS

Faith is taking the first step even when you don't see the whole staircase.

—MARTIN LUTHER KING, JR.

CHAPTER 9

THE MECCA

"Why would you choose Howard over Purdue? That's just stupid," my dad said. I remained silent and continued to gaze out the car window. Watching the houses whiz by, I leaned my head against the cold glass and tried to put as much distance between us as possible.

At this point, my relationship with my dad was beyond strained. But I still craved his approval and praise. Once again, I waited in vain for that to happen. And again, it was another dagger to my heart and spirit. Mostly, I pretended I didn't need him, but deep down, I still longed for a relationship with him.

Besides, I thought, as I sat brewing in silence, *he doesn't get to weigh in on my decision.* My mother had confessed to me and my sister that my dad spent our college savings years earlier to handle gambling debts after their divorce with no regret. When my mom confronted him, he haughtily told her the money came from his paycheck so he could spend it how he wanted despite their agreement to save for college tuition.

I couldn't stop the fire burning in my chest. *How could he do that to us?* I knew I couldn't bring this up to him now in the confines of the car. He would be pissed at my mom for telling us, and she would get the brunt of it. So, per usual, I didn't dare bring it up.

Early spring semester of my senior year of high school, I was still unsure about life after graduation. With my guidance counselor's encouragement, I took the Armed Services Vocational Aptitude Battery test at the beginning of that school year, but I knew the military wasn't for me. I didn't know where I fit, but I was easily influenced by Chief, and he ingrained the idea of attending college in my head. Chief, slowly but surely, began to convince me that not only was college for me but that I could run and compete at the collegiate level.

In his gruffy, bass voice, Chief proclaimed, "Hell, Desmond, you're going to college, and you're going to run, and you're going to pledge Alpha Phi Alpha. You're going to be a doctor, son. I know it." Because Chief said it, I accepted it. And when he suggested I attend Howard University, I ran with it.

I would have loved my dad's blessing in my college decision, but by this time in my life, Chief's words held more weight. Chief was my constant support. Chief showed up every day, encouraging me and challenging me to do better. He was the one who gave me a ride home from practice when it was too dark to walk by myself. He made sure I had something to eat when I didn't have cash to buy lunch. And he was at every meet—win, lose, or draw, he was there. My dad would be around for holidays and family reunions or gatherings, but he wasn't a daily presence to teach, encourage, discipline, and guide me.

I listened to my dad drone on and on and on in the car about how Purdue University is a good school and how it would be a huge mistake to go to an HBCU (historically Black college and university). He didn't know anyone who went to a HBCU, so he didn't believe Howard was good enough. Like most conversations with my dad, I didn't say much, and he didn't listen much. He thought telling me what to do based on his knowledge was the correct way to parent. He didn't make an effort to get to know me, to ask me questions about how I felt or what I liked. I was numb to his words. Relief flooded through me when we finally arrived at my grandfather's house, allowing me to jump out of the car and greet my family, who had gathered to celebrate my uncle's birthday, effectively ending the conversation.

After three attempts at taking the SATs, I finally landed the minimal standardized admission scores for Howard. I never visited the campus and initially learned about Howard from my mother's sister, Gwen, who was close friends with the provost for Howard. I didn't do the typical college visits and didn't apply to any schools except Purdue and Howard. No one guided me to choose several options, including a safe school and a stretch school, so I would have a variety of opportunities. The process was fairly simple for me. My aunt's connection got me in the door. As I walked into my grandfather's house and greeted my family, I tried to forget my father's words and reminded myself why I so adamantly chose Howard. I told myself I didn't care what he thought.

Three months later, I found myself sitting on a meager twin bed in my dorm room, struggling to breathe. I was on Howard's campus, in Washington, DC. The campus itself was a sprawling collection of brick buildings, some of which reminded me of office buildings and others that looked like smaller versions of my high school. The bright green athletic field sat adjacent to the building that housed the gymnasium. An open space was situated at the center of campus, about the size of a football field, that included trees and benches and walkways for students to gather. It was all perfectly inviting.

After finally slowing down my breathing, I wiped my face with the back of my hand and the collar of my T-shirt. I had been crying since the door slammed shut twenty minutes earlier. I struggled to keep my composure while my mom, Aunt Shirley, and I set up my tiny dorm room on the fifth floor of Charles Drew Hall. But I kept my emotions at bay by laughing and teasing my mom when she nagged me about making up my bed every day.

"Now, Dez, you're gonna have to keep your dirty clothes off the floor and keep all your toiletries in this shower basket," Mom directed me. I retorted with a few sarcastic comments, and she playfully slapped the back of my head. "And don't forget to separate your laundry. You can't wash the darks and lights together or else you'll ruin the whites."

With a playful look of frustration and an exasperated sigh, I said, "I know, Ma. You told me ten times already on the ride here!"

The banter continued as we organized my belongings into the drawers, baskets, and crates we picked up at K-Mart. Those moments were critical distractions from the pending water main break I held off until Mom was out of sight, on her way down the hallway, and headed back home to Gary.

I was overwhelmed and unnerved by the ferocity of my tears, but they were such a relief. Those tears needed to flow— to release the pent-up fear, anxiety, doubt, and confusion that were my unwelcomed companions during the eleven-hour ride from Gary, only growing more intense during the four hours we spent checking in and unpacking my dorm. She was gone. And now I was alone. And I was scared as hell.

Although my sister Shnicks had gone to college the year before me, I hadn't asked her enough questions about her experience. I didn't visit her on campus, so I had no idea what campus life was like. I didn't feel prepared at all.

Over the next few days, I got to know my roommate, Todd, and a few of the guys on my floor. One of those guys was Phillip McKenzie, who lived next door to me. Like me, Phil was also on the cross country and track team at Howard. Phil was from New York, and he was a smart dude with a ton of Brooklyn pride. We made it a habit to walk to and from practices together and usually ate lunch or dinner together in the cafe. Like most distance runners, Phil was slender and light on his feet. He was tall and well built, and though a handsome guy, I could tell he wasn't the partying type and took his studies seriously.

The more I got to know Phil and the more I interacted with other guys in my dorm, the more I realized how ill-equipped I was. They knew more about the world, about politics, about things I didn't even know mattered. Although I knew that Gary had some of the brightest and most talented minds, including those from my high school and in my graduating class, I couldn't ignore how the lack of resources and exposure growing up there grossly underprepared me for this level of academia. I didn't have conversations about current events in school. No one really asked me my opinion or views on global issues. I didn't have summer trips abroad to chat about and couldn't remember visiting museums or other cultural exhibitions. Howard was my first real introduction to life beyond Indiana.

Howard University, affectionately referred to as "The Mecca," is considered the most prestigious HBCU in the United States. "Mecca" refers to the city in Saudi Arabia, considered the holiest city in the Islamic religion. (Abdo and Glubb, 2021) Parallels between Mecca and Howard have been drawn because of the life-changing experiences students have during their time at Howard.

For decades since the Civil Rights Movement forced predominantly White colleges and universities to grant admissions to Blacks, there has been a debate about which types of institutions prepare African American students better for jobs, careers, and life after college. PWIs (predominantly White institutions) or HBCUs? Looking back, I'm sure my dad was not unlike so many Black people in this country, conditioned by Eurocentric culture to think that what is White is better, resulting in a feeling of inferiority. In his mind, of course, Purdue was the better choice. Because of systemic racism, at one point in history, Blacks could not be educated at all. In fact, it was a crime punishable by death. And then segregated schools were created, with minimal resources for the Black schools. Eventually HBCUs were founded as an attempt to provide higher education for the Black community when the all-White institutions denied us the opportunity. (OCR, 1991)

Howard, like other HBCUs, was known for providing Black students with the academic, emotional, and social support to manage the challenges of college life. For the first time in my life, I was a part of conversations in which my conventional beliefs were analyzed and challenged in classrooms, dorm rooms, the cafe, and campus open mics. There were times I learned just as much from late-night, deep discussions on the tile floors of my dorm hallways as I did in class. My eyes and ears were opened to another way of thinking—a way that affirmed who I was as a young Black man in America, whose rich history had been stripped, then pieced back together, bit by bit, on this historic and sacred campus. Phil, Todd, and other guys like Tim and Corey discussed topics I'd never thought about before, like obtaining assets, having financial investments, and being an entrepreneur and owner versus being solely a consumer.

"Man, Black people have to realize our collective power. If we came together to purchase real estate and businesses, we could hire our own people and then reinvest in our own communities . . . giving all of us an equal opportunity to succeed in life."

"But the system isn't designed to give us those opportunities. We just don't have enough generational wealth. Redlining made sure of that!"

"Yeah, but too many of us move out of the 'hood and never come back. We gotta be the ones to bring up the next generation. How can we do that if we get ours and then move out to the suburbs and never reach back?"

These guys had short-term and long-term academic and career goals. They felt responsible for not only their lives, but also for impacting their communities. They felt connected to a bigger cause for change. As young Black men, they felt both the pressure and the power.

Many of our discussions turned to our survival as young Black men. Whether it was being profiled in a department store or being profiled by the police, we all had stories we swapped about what we had to do to simply stay alive and free from incarceration. When these topics came up, I often thought about my childhood friends who didn't make it, who were violently killed by gun violence for reasons including being at the wrong place at the wrong time, to mistaken identity, to adolescent mistakes, and silly beefs. I still think about Ron-Ron, Mark, and Jeremy, who all lived within a block of my childhood home.

Unlike what I heard from friends who went to big state schools and predominantly White universities, I was more than a number at Howard. I belonged to a community designed for me, and I felt special. Professors knew my name and were eager to help me during their office hours.

I didn't rub it in my dad's face, but it made me proud to have stuck with my decision to attend Howard instead of succumbing to his pressure to go to Purdue.

I chose pre-engineering as my major and quickly found myself spending late nights in the engineering lab. This was not a place where I could coast or slack off in the last row, as I did in Ms. Smith's English class in high school. Luckily, I had Phil to help support me along the way.

Although he was a finance major, we often studied together and ensured we didn't miss any classes except when we were away for cross country meets that fall. Phil went to a highly competitive high school in Brooklyn and was confident in his academic preparation. He was focused and knew much about our culture and our history as Black people. In a short amount of time, I learned so much from Phil. He was highly focused, well organized, and goal oriented. Even on the track team, I quickly observed he was a fierce competitor. He was the type of guy I wanted and needed to be around.

One sunny fall afternoon on the way back from cross country practice, Phil and I noticed a flier advertising an interest meeting for a social club called Gentlemen of Drew. Gentlemen of Drew, or G.O.D. for short, was a club that provided an opportunity for freshman boys in our dorm to bond and support one another. G.O.D. was named after our outdated dorm, Drew Hall, which was named for Charles

Drew, the African American surgeon who developed ways to store plasma in blood banks. (Biography.com, 2020) The flier captured my interest, and I was excited to learn more about it. Phil had no interest in becoming a part of G.O.D. He was more interested in spending time with a young lady who was a freshman at Georgetown University, a few miles across town, whom he had met and started dating within the first month of classes.

I was intrigued by the idea of being a part of a community. I missed the camaraderie of my high school teammates and hadn't yet bonded in that way with my new team at Howard. I felt as if I needed a place to belong because deep down, I didn't feel like I measured up to the other students on campus.

At the G.O.D. interest meeting, I listened to the sophomore and junior guys, who had joined the club during their freshman year, speak confidently and proudly. They talked about G.O.D. being like a brotherhood and how proud they were of the hours of community service they did together. And I wanted in.

I submitted my application and was soon called for an interview. At the interview, I found myself, again, feeling completely unprepared. I sat in a chair in front of a row of five guys, all dressed in ties and slacks and suit jackets. The panel of men who interrogated me were just a year or two older than me, but it felt as if they were wiser and more experienced by decades. I fumbled my way through two rounds of interviews. I was sweating profusely, and my mouth felt like it was filled with cotton, and when my mind was thinking of one answer, it would quickly translate to another that would make no sense coming out of my mouth.

"What kind of change do you think is necessary to liberate the Black community?" a sophomore with a bald head and bushy eyebrows asked.

"Uh, Black communities need better schools?" I responded with uncertainty. "They need teachers who can teach, and, uh, we need to stop killin' one another and stop the violence. . . ." My mind was so frazzled and jumbled I couldn't finish half of my responses throughout the round.

The G.O.D. brothers highlighted my fumbles, snickering at times and keeping their faces stoic at other times.

"You got a long way to go, brutha," commented the guy in the middle of the panel with a paisley tie and close-cut fade.

"For real," co-signed the stocky, fair-skinned brother on the end of the row of panelists, shaking his head in disappointment.

Massive flames of uncertainty ignited about who I was and who I could become.

After the interviewing process, I felt deflated. A few days later, I received my rejection letter. Again, I didn't make the cut, but now the stakes felt higher. Learning there was a ninety-eight percent acceptance rate, I was devastated to be the odd man out. I despised some of the leaders because they mocked my unpreparedness. I didn't feel the love, the mentorship, and the leadership I expected based on what was presented at the interest meeting. This didn't feel like brotherhood.

I'd been here before. I faced rejection from my father as a child. I faced rejection when I tried out for my middle school cross country team. Rejection was not a final fate for me. I knew it was important for me to move on and continue to focus on my academic and running goals. If I wanted to achieve anything of value, shortcuts would not be involved.

G.O.D. or not, I knew I could not afford to stay discouraged. I would find my home, the friends and guys who I could connect with, who I could look up to. I needed to find my team, my brotherhood again, and I wouldn't let rejection deter me.

CHAPTER 10

EYES WIDE OPEN

———

I knew that finding my crew—my brothers—would be important for me to feel at home at Howard. I wasn't sure where I would find that brotherhood, but I knew it was necessary. A huge part of my identity was connected to the village that raised me and supported me. It was the village that got me to Howard. That village included my family and Chief and my high school team. Because none of those people were here with me at school, I needed to recreate that village.

At the end of the orientation week of my freshman year, I met one of the coolest and sharpest guys who had ever walked Howard's campus, Charles Graham. Charles was a mentor in an organization called Campus Pals. The university set up this organization to provide incoming students with an upperclassman who could support and mentor them during their critical first year on campus. My orientation letter said Charles was assigned as my "Pal."

I met Charles at the annual Campus Pals ice cream social, the end-of-week celebration culminating freshman orientation. Phil and I were excited to hang out and meet other freshmen to ease the anxiety building as we headed into our first week of classes.

"Hey, Dez, nice to meet you," Charles said with a wide grin.

He was shorter than me, about five feet, eight inches tall, but his confidence and presence made him seem like a giant. He was funny, cool, and down to earth. He was smart, eloquent, compassionate, and driven, but never pretentious or obnoxious. And he was the president of Alpha Phi Alpha Fraternity, Inc., Beta Chapter.

Alpha is the first Black Greek letter fraternity in America, founded at Cornell University in 1906. Alpha's Beta Chapter was the first to be chartered at a HBCU. Alpha boasts some of the most dynamic leaders in the Black community, including Jesse Owens, Garrett Morgan, Chaka Fattah, Martin Luther King Jr., Ralph Bunche, Andrew Young, Thurgood Marshall, Duke Ellington, Stuart Scott, and Stan Verrett. (Alpha Phi Alpha Fraternity, Inc., 2021) With this legacy, I knew Charles had to be somebody special.

Charles soon became my role model and the person I aspired to emulate. Charles and his Alpha fraternity brothers heightened my interest in a formalized brotherhood after witnessing the love, camaraderie, and leadership these Black men displayed around campus. Their greetings to one another, with secret handshakes, hugs, and fraternity chants, reflected a connection to something bigger than who they were as individuals. They wore black and gold T-shirts, jackets and hats, the paraphernalia making them easily recognizable. But their presence on campus, their confidence in classes, and their pursuit for excellence were most influential.

A couple of months after I met Charles, after my rejection from G.O.D., he invited me to one of the programs his fraternity was hosting featuring an author named Anthony Browder. When I arrived that evening, I walked into the meeting room in Blackburn Student Center and immediately felt underdressed in my jeans, polo shirt, and loafers. All the brothers of Alpha Phi Alpha wore slacks and ties, and many of them wore suits. They seemed so sure of themselves, so professional. So, I tried to wipe my hands on my jeans to minimize the clamminess forming on my palms. I introduced myself to a few of the guys and took my seat.

Over the next forty-five minutes, Anthony Browder discussed the power of Black men and the history of our people.

I remember him saying, "We come from a powerful people. We created civilizations. The media wants to portray us like we come from barbaric people. That's simply not true. The innovation and sophistication of our ancient African civilizations provided the foundation for all modern societies today."

I have never heard anybody talk like this before, I thought. *Where did he learn all this? I want to know what he knows.*

He went on to speak vigorously about the impact of our words and how we can use them to manifest things in our lives. I left intrigued not only by how smart and confident Browder was but also by how he challenged my thinking and offered alternative beliefs about who I was as a Black man. This was not something I learned from school, even though Gary's population was 81 percent Black. (US Census, 1990) He was the most powerful speaker I had ever heard.

The energy and brotherly love in the room were magnetic. The brothers listened intently to Browder, nodding their heads when they agreed with his sentiments and exchanging knowing glances when Browder said something that intrigued them. They worked together, organizing the question-and-answer dialogue and even serving us refreshments at the end of the event. I left feeling empowered, as if

I learned more in that one night about who I really was than I had learned in my whole life.

I began to realize fraternal bonds were deeper than the collegiality I observed. Their mission was to develop leaders and promote brotherhood and academic excellence while providing service and advocacy for our communities and beyond.

* * *

By early winter of my freshman year, I was getting my sea legs under me on campus. I began to develop friendships. I knew what it meant to study and prioritize my academics. I had a vision for what true brotherhood could look like in a fraternity and knew I wanted to pledge Alpha when I was eligible during my sophomore year. And I finally found my new team: Track Bison.

I was blessed to be given a partial athletic scholarship to run track at Howard and immediately found support in the team atmosphere.

At many NCAA Division I programs, student-athletes felt incredible pressure to perform or risk losing scholarships. Fortunately, I didn't feel that way. Our legendary coach, William P. Moultrie, focused on making us better people. Coach Moultrie was a country boy at heart. Born and raised in Rockdale, Texas, he wore his cowboy boots and big belt buckle proudly. Moultrie became an assistant coach for the 1992 Olympic team and then made history as the first African American Olympic track referee at the 1996 Atlanta Olympic Games. (USTFCCCA n.d.)

Coach Moultrie was about six feet, one inch, but because he always wore a cowboy hat, he appeared taller. His skin tone was a deep brown, usually tanned even more because he spent so much time outside on the track. His presence was booming, and he walked with purpose. He was far from a pushover; in fact, he was often more of a brutal, in-your-face, "tell it like it is," and "hurt your feelings" kind of coach. But we always felt his southern hospitality and his love.

He was a leader, a trailblazer, a mentor we all looked up to. We bought into his willingness and obligation to build character more than win championships. He pushed us athletically, that was for sure, but he challenged us to hold ourselves and one another accountable. He made it imperative that we represent the team and the university at the highest level and make a difference and pave the way for those coming up behind us. Most of all, he demanded that we respect ourselves and represent our families in the most honorable fashion.

Couch Moultrie's philosophy was made clear to me at one of my first cross country meets. Where most freshmen traveled to local meets around DC, Phil and I were the only two freshmen to make the travel racing team after finishing with times ranking us in the top seven at previous meets. Phil and I were excited about our first travel meet, and after classes Friday, the day before the meet, we packed our duffel bags and made our way to the fifteen-passenger van parked next to Burr Gymnasium. A few of our teammates gathered outside the van, chatting and waiting for Coach Moultrie to come out from his office on the bottom level of Burr. Phil and I walked up and greeted our teammates Reggie Johnson, Shaun Bell, Jomo Davis, and Thomas C. Smith.

We chatted a bit, enjoying the mild weather on the late fall afternoon. The last of our teammates joined us as we eagerly waited to start our road trip. Coach Moultrie came striding out of Burr, wearing his usual beige cowboy hat and dark brown boots.

"All right guys, let's load up," he said. Phil and I grabbed our bags and climbed into the van after Thomas.

"On the hump, freshmen," Thomas said and nodded to the rise in the floor between the second and third row of the van.

"Oh, hell no, I ain't sittin' there," Phil replied.

"You're a freshman. You sit where I say you sit," Thomas responded back.

The other upperclassmen chimed in.

"Yeah, on the hump, freshmen!"

"Gotta pay your dues, freshmen!"

I tapped Phil and mumbled, "Man, let's just sit here for now. This ain't no big deal." I could tell Phil was fuming, but he complied. Coach Moultrie finally drove us off, and we headed about an hour away, just on the other side of Baltimore. The guys joked and laughed on the ride. Phil didn't say much the entire time. I didn't either. My loyalty was to Phil, but I knew I couldn't help him win the battle against those upperclassmen.

The next day, our showing at the Morgan State Invitational was worth the uncomfortable ride. We dominated the field, and Phil not only led our team, but he also won the entire race! *Yeah, now they have to respect freshmen who can run like that!* We chatted proudly and excitedly, joking around as we made our way back to the van to head home after the awards ceremony ended.

"I'm pumped!" I said to Phil with a bounce in my step.

"Man, we can be really good this year," Reggie said as we got closer to the van.

"Yeah, we can actually win our conference championships," Jomo chimed in. "Good job, freshmen," he said, nodding toward us. Phil and I nodded in agreement, not yet really knowing the magnitude of such a win. We climbed back into the van, eager to grab a comfortable seat for the ride back, especially because we were exhausted and our legs still felt like Jell-O.

"Oh no, freshmen. Back on the hump," Thomas said.

"Hell, naw!" Phil rebuked. "I just beat all y'all. I ain't sittin' back on that thing. Shit, one of you needs to sit there."

"Who the hell you talkin' to, freshman?!" Thomas retorted. "You betta back yo' ass down before you get beat down!"

Phil was not phased, "What you gonna do, fool? I done told you I ain't sittin' on the damn hump!"

Coach Moultrie heard the ruckus and was not happy.

"Son, come here," he said gruffly to Phil. The two of them walked away from the van, outside of earshot from the rest of us.

Phil told me that Coach Moultrie reiterated that his team was about respect and teamwork and that he would not tolerate the kind of talk that he heard from Phil. When Phil tried to defend himself, Coach Moultrie dismissed Phil's arguments, reiterating that Phil needed to pay his dues and carry himself with more respect. Coach Moultrie didn't yell or use foul language, but Phil knew he had to fall in line. Coach Moultrie was not one to be tested.

As Moultrie walked away, I overheard him say to Phil, "Gold doesn't shine until it goes through the fire!"

On the ride back, Phil was pissed again as we sat in silence. I didn't agree with this hierarchy rule that put us at a disadvantage as freshmen. I believed age and years didn't matter as much as effort. *This is bullshit.* But I didn't dare say a word. Not yet.

Although that bus ride home was far from ideal, we didn't let it sour our attitude about being a part of the Track Bison family. As a team, we all kept plugging away at practices. And I didn't hold back when it came to challenging my teammates. On one long run, my teammate Corey got so winded that he stopped.

As Phil and I approached him, my puzzled and concerned look grew to fury and anger as I got closer. With his hands on his knees, Corey was simply out of breath, not injured or hurt like I initially thought.

"Come on, man!" I yelled at him. Grabbing him under his chin, I lifted him up and repeated myself, "Come on, man! We're trying to win MEACs this year!" I reminded him we had a chance to actually win the Mid-Eastern Athletic Conference title, which we had never done as a program. Again, I yelled at Corey, "Let's go, man!"

Corey took a deep breath and raised up tall. He looked at me and Phil, knowing we would not leave him alone. He shook his head and then slowly trotted behind us, regaining some speed in his stride after a few paces.

I quickly earned the reputation of being no-nonsense at practice. I didn't hesitate to call out my teammates if they tried to slack off. The culture Chief had built for my high school team was what I practiced. Intense work ethic. High accountability. No excuses. And my Howard teammates began to notice those traits throughout my freshman year.

Although I was a workhorse, I was not as talented as several of the other guys, including Phil. Phil was not only talented, but he also came from a high school program that was highly competitive. Brooklyn Tech won a state championship and a triple crown (winning conference cross country, indoor, and outdoor track titles) in Phil's senior year, and he was always quick to remind you he came from a winning team.

The upperclassmen tolerated Phil's ego, just a bit, because he continued to lead us, finishing first or second to Reggie on the team in nearly every meet. Leading up to the MEAC championships, we were confident that with Phil and Reggie paving the way, we would snag the first conference championship in school history.

By the time we lined up for the conference championship race, we had gelled as a team, and although I missed my boys from Horace Mann, I loved running for Howard and exuded newfound swag when I put on that HU jersey.

I looked down the starting line, nervous but confident. Our competing teams were not unfamiliar to us, with the exception of Florida A&M, but I couldn't predict the outcome. Morgan State's number one guy and our top two guys had battled before, and our guys had enough in their tank to beat him. I was sure of it. We all were. The rest of us would be their supporting cast, with enough strength to place well and win the overall team award.

Sweat trickled down my back and across my forehead. It was a crisp fall day in early November, but our warmup was thorough. I was ready.

"Runners, set," the starter called out. Everyone leaned forward, crouching in starting position, tension building.

Pow! And we were sprinting forward on the green-beige grass. I quickly found my rhythm, settling into the middle of the pack and watching Phil and Reggie ahead of me. I knew they would be ahead of me, and I knew I was responsible for having their backs, doing my part to stay close enough to keep the point spread as narrow as possible.

After the first mile through the tree-lined course, I could barely see the lead, but I was trailing the huge chase pack, which is the group of runners close behind the leaders of the race. I kept close and strategically maneuvered around any runner who was immediately in front of me when I was able. This was a ten-kilometer race (6.2 miles), so I settled in, relying on my years of endurance and conditioning.

By mile three, the heavy breathing around me became my soundtrack. I ignored the tightness in my chest and stayed focused on the next group ahead of me, pumping my arms with more effort, still feeling comfortable enough to surge past the next runner a few strides in front of me. I looked up, and I was now connecting with my teammates in the top twenty. Strength comes in numbers, and we were strong.

It was our second rodeo up "Parachute Hill," given the nickname for its length and sharp, drastic incline, and it was the perfect time to make up ground. I capitalized, and so did my teammates.

At the apex of the hill, three race marshals waved us to the right.

Ahead of me, I couldn't see Phil's battle, but I knew he was out there. We were gunning for Morgan State, hoping for Phil and Reggie to be our one-two punch for the victory.

I finished the race with a strong kick, inching past one more of my opponents, determined to score as low as possible as one of our top seven.

I stumbled out of the finish-line chute and found a couple of my teammates a few feet away. Reggie was on the ground, head between his knees, trying to catch his breath. Phil was stumbling around, extremely upset.

"This is bullshit, man!" He sputtered between gasps. I had no idea what he was talking about but couldn't ask questions yet. I was still struggling to breathe and stand at the same time. I threw a cup of water that I grabbed from the table at the end of the finish line on my head . My hands then moved to my head to open up my lungs, which were desperately begging for more air.

After a few more minutes, I was able to trudge closer to Phil.

"Phil, what's wrong, man? How'd you finish?" I asked.

"Man, they let us go the wrong way. I was out front. Then . . . we . . . man, we went . . . the wrong way!"

"Huh?" was all I could muster at first. "What, what do you mean?"

"We went the wrong way! Me and the Florida A&M guy. Then they sent us back, but like ten guys had already gone past. We ran like 400 meters extra . . . shit!" Phil looked ready to cry. Or explode. Or both.

As I pieced together what he said, it was clear that while leading the race, Phil and his opponent had gone the wrong way, and once they were directed back onto the course, they had too much ground to make up to catch the front pack of runners.

I didn't have a response. *So, what did this mean? Where did he place? Were our championship hopes dashed?*

We huddled as a team after putting on our sweatpants to await the results. The announcer raised his megaphone to his lips and began calling out the final scores and team awards.

"In fourth place, with 107 points, North Carolina A&T. In third place, with seventy-one points, Florida A&M . . ."

My stomach was turning, so I put my head down to say a little prayer.

"And in second place, with seventy points, Howard. And in first place, by just three points, Morgan State, with sixty-seven total points!"

I lifted my head and took a deep breath. Then I looked over at Phil. He looked crushed. I knew he felt culpable for this loss. Thomas, Jomo, and Broderick Harrell went to the awards table to claim our team plaque. The rest of us tried our best to smile during the team photo. Runner-up wasn't bad. It was our best showing as a school in a while. Moultrie told us he was proud of us and that we should be, too. I wanted to feel that pride he spoke of, but I couldn't quite muster it. We left something out there on the course, as if someone grabbed it before we could retrieve what was rightfully ours.

Although the loss hurt, this was confirmation for me. I ached because I had not done more for my teammates. A shift had taken place. I finally found a home I craved after much trial and error, a new team of brothers I wanted to run for, and who would shape this next journey in my life.

CHAPTER 11

LOSING MY FOOTING

———

My freshman year flew by, and after a solid spring outdoor track season, I headed home for the summer. I filled those summer weeks working a part-time job, getting in my mileage with long runs, and hanging out with my former teammates and high school friends. Before I knew it, the first semester of my sophomore year rolled around. I jumped back into my routine of classes and cross country practices. Within a few weeks, I shifted my focus to following in the footsteps of my new mentor Charles Graham. I began to seriously pursue membership in Alpha Phi Alpha.

Phil and I both expressed interest in the fraternity, and we began to attend programs Alpha Phi Alpha sponsored on campus. The programs included educational and cultural workshops, community service events, and social mixers. We sought to get to know other members of Alpha, including Charles Graham, Darrius Gourdine, Kevin Monroe, and Ronald Sullivan, and the more we did, the more I realized I craved the mentorship and leadership the older brothers could provide. The need for a sense of belonging, beyond what I formed with my Track Bison teammates, was drawing me in further.

While Phil and I seriously pursued membership, we met other pledges with the same mentality. But, boy, were they ahead of the pack. Brett Allen, a fair-skinned, curly brown-haired guy from Detroit was one of them. He and Joey Gibbs stood in front of our hopeful group, which had assembled in a dorm basement on campus. Joey was a few inches shorter than me but seemed to stand above us all with knowledge that none of us possessed. He was muscular, built like a fullback, and spoke with a slight Southern twang and conviction about what we should do and expect during this prospective process. We soon found out that Joey's brother was a member of Alpha and had pledged a year earlier.

"We need to get to know every brother on campus. Those who have graduated, call them up . . . any of the brothers who have pledged in the last ten years," Joey began. "Be seen but not seen. Go to your classes, your practices, the workshops and programs, but don't be seen at any parties. This process is now a priority in our lives, and we don't have time to socialize." Joey paused and gazed intensely at us. We were solemn, taking it all in.

He continued, "Here are the parts of the history you need to learn. Know the founding brothers, known as the Seven Jewels. Learn all the single-letter chapters . . ."

Joey captivated us, and we were hungry for the information. As he doled out more, we all listened quietly and intently. Some of us leaned in, as if that slight action would deepen our understanding. Others took notes, scribbling as fast as possible, capturing as much detail as was shared. It was the beginning of our covert operation. We would be a part of a secret society on campus until we learned all we needed to know and proved our devotion and commitment. Then—and only if we had earned it—would we be invited to join the oldest, most prestigious, Black-founded fraternity on any college campus.

Phil and I quickly fell into an intense routine in our pursuit of Alpha. We attended all our classes each day. We attended practice after classes. And then we spent the evenings studying our Alpha history and information, getting to know the current members of Alpha and mingling with the other guys seeking membership. Phil and I connected with Brett and Joey more frequently and we soon began to spend most of our time in the group. We spent so much of our free time pursuing Alpha that we had little time to study for our classes. So much so that Brett, Joey and I found ourselves in a position that we hadn't expected. We lost focus. We lost our way and fumbled our academic priorities. Our fall semester grades were so dismal that we no longer had the GPA to be eligible to pledge in the spring.

I was juggling so much during the fall semester—classes, pledging, and practice—that, by the time December arrived, I couldn't wait for winter break. Getting back home and spending time with my family did me well. Enjoying my mom's home-cooked meals, playing cards into the wee hours of the night with my cousins, and laying around the house with my mom and Shnicks felt rejuvenating.

During the winter break, I was able to recharge and train with my old high school team. Chief always let alumni hop into the workouts over the breaks, and it was affirming to still feel connected to the team that had been like family to me for so many years. Chief even put an eleven-by-fourteen photo of me in my Howard uniform in the high school gym trophy case, making me stick my chest out a little more when I visited my alma mater. Many of the younger guys still on the team looked up to me. Going back was like a reunion. It was comforting, both emotionally and physically. It was home.

The counselors at my old high school also invited me to talk to students about attending college. I looked forward to the responsibility of encouraging others to pursue higher education and to be a role model. I made a lot of people proud but also made myself proud in the process.

On my second day back on campus after the break, I woke up at 6 a.m., got dressed and ready to catch the bus for our first indoor track meet. I walked from my dorm, Carver Hall, in the dark with a cluster of my teammates. We chatted loosely on the roughly six-block walk to the stadium where the bus waited. As we were throwing our bags under the bus, Coach Moultrie stepped off it with a pen and a pad. He looked down at it again and then looked up at me.

"Desmond. Come here, son." I walked closer to Coach.

"You can't come with us. Your grades from last semester weren't too good, I see. You're not able to travel with the team." Shaking his head, he continued to peer at me.

"Son, you told me you wanted to be here. Get your bag, and we'll continue this conversation in a couple days."

My heart sank. With my head down, I grabbed my bag. I knew my grades weren't looking too hot, but it was not until that moment that it really hit me. I watched the bus roll away and imagined my scholarship and my life as a college student at Howard slipping away.

The long walk back to my dorm felt like a march of death. *How did I mess this up?* I had such a successful freshman year but had fallen quickly by the middle of the fall semester of my sophomore year. After I met Charles Graham and sat in the audience when Anthony Browder spoke, I yearned to be an Alpha man. The fraternity could provide me with a lifelong brotherhood outside of my Track Bison, but there would be no fraternity for me if I didn't keep my eyes on my academics and stay in school. The pre-pledge period—learning the history of the fraternity and getting to know the brotherhood—consumed me. I wasn't partying like many people do in college, but I prioritized other opportunities over my classes, and as admirable as that was, I knew I had to recommit and bring up my failing grades.

How am I going to tell Ma and Chief? What will happen if I'm sent home? What will my family say? With every step back toward my dorm, I grew more and more upset. *How did I let this happen? What if I can't bring my grades up?* I fought back the tears that burned in my eyes and threatened to spill over. My pace quickened as my nose began to run, the crisp January air burning the insides of my nostrils. I didn't want anyone to see the defiant tears that refused to stay hidden in my tear ducts.

Once I got to my dorm room, I threw one of my books across the room and collapsed on the bed in an ugly, desperate cry. Snot and all.

That night, I couldn't sleep. Moments from the last semester replayed in my head. There were so many times when I went to class so tired that I knew I didn't take good notes and I knew I didn't comprehend the lecture. Once the pre-pledge period began, my organized classwork schedule was neglected, and I began spending so much free time preparing for the spring pledge process that I no longer prioritized my education. I still went to my classes, but my studying was inconsistent, and my attention in class was minimal. I squeezed by and earned a passing grade in the elective course outside my major, but my required courses suffered.

Determined to fix this situation, I met with my academic advisor to see how I could get back on course. She just shook her head when I told her that I knew I wasn't doing well, but I had no idea that one poor semester would leave me ineligible and in danger of being dismissed from the university. She told me I could take two courses in summer school. I couldn't afford to take the classes at Howard but discovered I could take them at my hometown community college, Indiana University Northwest—a little sliver of hope for turning things around.

I set up a meeting with Coach Moultrie that same week. My heart was pounding, and my stomach turned as I walked into his office. He was sitting at his large wooden desk with his hands locked across his chest.

"Son, your mother has done a lot to make sure you got here. Not everyone is given these types of opportunities. I'm disappointed. This is something you're going to have to figure out. Not everyone is meant to be a Track Bison. A third of the students that come here don't graduate. It's hard to get in, but it's even harder to graduate, and even harder to be a Track Bison."

He continued, "You're ineligible, son. And that means you can't keep your scholarship." His gaze intensified, and his frown deepened.

Those words echoed in my ears. *You can't keep your scholarship.* "What do you mean?" I asked, confused.

He leaned forward and propped his elbows on his desk. His voice became slightly louder and sharp as he said, "I can't give you any athletic financial aid. You didn't hold up your end of the bargain." I sat for a few moments in silence and disbelief. Eventually, I pulled myself from the chair and slowly headed for the door.

As soon as I left the office, tears started, and I couldn't regain my composure on the trek home across campus.

That evening, I knew I had to call my mom to give her the news. There was no way to put that off. The phone rang, and I hoped she wouldn't pick up. But on the second ring my hopes were dashed.

"Hello?" she answered.

"Hey, Ma."

"Hey, fella, how ya doing'?" she asked. I gripped my phone tighter as I sat on my twin bed. My stomach was in knots as I searched for the right words to start the conversation.

"Fella?" she said again. Hearing the nickname she gave me as a little boy made my heart sink even more, knowing I would disappoint her with the news I called to share.

"I'm here. I gotta tell you something, Ma," I began. "I, uh, I lost my scholarship," I finally blurted out.

My mom sighed into the phone. "Oh, Dez . . . how?" I tried to explain why I had missed some classes and failed some exams, but it didn't make sense hearing it out loud.

She sighed again. "I can't help you with this," she said. "You made your bed, and you gotta lay in it and figure this one out. I don't have any money to waste."

I knew she was right. I thought about what Chief always said to our team in high school: "You can take the rest of the day to wallow in your misery, but when that sun comes up the next day, true champions pick their head up and get back to it." I had no idea how I would dig myself out of this one, but I knew I had to try.

That spring semester, I had to train on my own instead of with the team. Some of the guys I grew to know during the Alpha pre-pledge period continued on to the pledge process. I was now torn from both sets of brothers I grew to depend on—my teammates and my friends who also sought to be Alpha men. The entire semester continued in a lackluster fashion.

For the first time, my mother had truly cut the cord. She offered no financial help to compensate for my lost scholarship. At the end of the spring semester, I knew I needed to go back home and pursue a summer job at the East Chicago Boys & Girls Club to pay for my summer courses. I took out loans for the upcoming fall semester to cover the loss of my scholarship. I figured out my own training regimen for the summer. I had to train twice a day, morning and evening, because I couldn't get in all my miles before work and classes. While most college students were hanging out over the summer, going to the movies and parties, I was spending six days a week waking up at 5:30 a.m. to run on my old high school's track, logging anywhere from five to ten miles. My summer school classes started at 8:30 a.m. and ended at noon. I worked from 1 to 7 p.m., then headed back to the track to finish the day with a short run, typically three to five miles.

I had something to prove to my mom. To Chief. To Coach Moultrie. To myself. But I was exhausted. This summer was different from the previous one where I had independence and freedom as a young adult. I was on a mission now. I was on a grind.

Later in the summer, I called Coach Moultrie to give him updates on my progress. Before I could give him all the details about what I had been up to over the summer, he said, "Son, we're going to have to talk face to face about this. We need to have a longer conversation, and I need to know you're back on the right track."

CHAPTER 12

FINDING REDEMPTION

As soon as I stepped foot on campus in mid-August, my first stop was the office of the director of residential life. I called all summer to inquire about being a resident assistant (RA). I was told all the positions had been filled, but that didn't deter me from calling. The director was impressed with my tenacity but still said there wasn't an open spot.

A week later, I received a call from residence life. One of the RAs they had secured was suddenly not returning. The woman on the phone asked whether I was still interested. I jumped on the opportunity. The RA position meant my housing would be taken care of financially. Residence life was also concerned about my grades, but I explained I could relate to the students' challenges and that, because of my adversity, I would better be able to help the residents.

Next, I had to figure out tuition. I decided to go see Ms. Baskerville in the bursar's office. I was introduced to her by a family friend who worked in the provost's office on campus and was advised to see her if I ever had issues. But meeting with her required even more persistence than I needed to become an RA.

I stood in line for about four hours with all the other students trying to get registered for classes.

I finally reached the front of the line and greeted Ms. Baskerville, one of the administrators responsible for registration and financial aid. She reminded me of an old-school, but still hip, aunt. She wore stylish glasses and had a light-brown complexion and black hair she usually pulled back in a bun at the nape of her neck.

"How you doin', honey?" she asked as I approached.

"I'm okay, but I lost my scholarship, and I'm trying to get registered." I looked down and shifted my weight uncomfortably.

"Oh, no. How'd you manage to do that?" She asked with a fury in her brow.

"I was trying to pledge . . ." my voice trailed off, and I couldn't bring myself to look at her directly.

Her look told me she wasn't sure she could help.

"I have a work-study job now, and I'm an RA, but it's just not enough." I couldn't quite hold it together, and the tears started to flow. I looked around sheepishly to see whether anyone was looking at me.

She took a deep breath and peered at me through her glasses. "I want to help, and I'll do what I can to buy you some time, but with this outstanding bill, you won't be able to register for the spring semester." I had no choice but to be hopeful. Plus, I had more confidence and a strong handle on time management from my brutal summer at home. I dug deep with dogged focus. When I saw the track team training, regret instinctively followed, but the next moment, I found the incredible resolve to work my butt off so I could earn my spot back on the team.

I even attempted the pre-pledge process with Alpha again, the familiarity of the process from last year aiding me in the attempt. My work ethic stepped up in all aspects of my life.

A couple of months later, I stopped by to see Ms. Baskerville in her office to update her on how I was doing.

"I'm so glad you're doing better in your classes," she praised with a smile.

I continued on and told her my training was going okay, but I had lost so much momentum from last year. She encouraged me to keep working hard. I told her I was probably going to need to take out more loans for the next semester. She got up for a minute, and when she came back, she handed me a piece of paper.

At the top of the paper, I saw my name, and at the bottom, I saw a balance of zero dollars. My eyes widened. Immediately, I jumped up from the wooden chair with a huge grin.

"Thank you, thank you!" I exclaimed.

She replied, "We just got a grant for students who have a certain GPA, and because of your summer classes, you meet the qualifications. Here's an early Christmas present."

I continued to thank her profusely and then turned to leave. She lightly touched my arm and leaned in, "Don't tell anybody, now," she whispered. As I write this book, I'm sure she's retired, so I don't think she will mind me sharing this story of her tremendous generosity.

It was by far the nicest thing anyone had ever done for me. I walked through the lobby and pumped my fist as if I had won a championship game. I practically skipped across the yard and to the cafeteria where I met up with some friends. They wondered why I was so happy, but I honored my promise to Ms. Baskerville and kept the good news to myself. For the first time in a long time, I felt lighter. I could really turn things around.

* * *

When we met in person upon my return to campus for junior year, Coach Moultrie gave me an ultimatum: If I received a 3.0 GPA my junior year, he would return my scholarship for my senior year. If not, my scholarship was gone for good.

I struggled not to cave under the pressure of earning back my scholarship. My grades needed to be my priority, and I felt as if I owed the team. My teammates depended on me, and I had become the weak link in the chain.

I headed to Coach Moultrie's office on the first Monday of spring semester. The closer I walked to Burr Gymnasium, the location of his office, the faster my heartbeat. Rubbing my hands nervously on my pants, I opened the building door and walked downstairs, down the intimidating stretch of hallway to his office. I knocked and waited for him to respond.

"Come in," came his thunderous voice.

As I opened the door, he greeted me from his desk chair.

"Hey, Desmond." Per usual, his beige cowboy hat sat atop his head.

"Hey, Coach," I said just a few decibels louder than the heartbeat I could hear pulsating at my temples. "I came by to share my good news." I paused, but when he didn't respond, I continued. "I brought my grades up last semester, and my GPA is now over a 3.0. I was hoping I could join the team again."

Coach Moultrie leaned back in his chair and continued his intense gaze. He clasped his hands at his midsection and took a breath before speaking. "Well, son, I'm glad you got your grades up. But you really let down the team. How do I know you're not going to do that again?"

"I know, Coach. I know. I really got caught up and lost my focus. But I won't let that happen again. I've been working hard to get my grades back up, and I went to summer school to make up those credits I missed. And I've been training on my own every day, so I'm still in good shape." I paused and waited anxiously for a response.

"Uh, huh," he uttered. I waited for another three seconds, but the silence was suffocating. I peered past his face and looked out the window behind him, noticing a few students scurrying to class.

I continued to stumble through my plea, "Yeah, and, uh, I really want to be back on the team, and I guarantee I will work harder than ever. I know I messed up, but I learned my lesson, Coach."

"Uh, huh." Another pause. Nothing more. A bird landed on the windowsill outside.

"Coach, I have to get back on the team. I don't know what I'll do without running and the team. It means everything to me." I wiped my palms on my jogging pants again, but it didn't help the clamminess. My stomach churned waiting for Coach to consider my fate. The bird took flight, leaving me alone to face Coach as my fate rested snuggly in his hands.

He continued to stare at me, then sat up and leaned his elbows on his desk. He cleared his throat. "Desmond, you're a good guy. And you're a hard worker. But you have to keep your priorities straight. You know how many guys like you wish they were here at Howard? Don't mess this up for yourself."

I sat up straighter. "Yes, sir. I won't." I let just a tiny bit of hope creep in.

A few seconds passed. More seconds went by. "Okay. I'll see you at practice tomorrow," Coach said with his hands clasped on his lap and relaxing back in his chair.

I jumped up feeling twenty pounds lighter. "Thank you, Coach! I won't let you down!" Coach kept a stern look on his face, daring me to drop the ball again. I nearly ran out of his office, but I didn't feel my feet touch the ground. Once I got outside, I leaped into the air. "Yes, yes, yes!"

I then found myself juggling classes, track practice, and the process of pledging Alpha. Joey, Brett, and I were three of eighteen pledgees who embarked on the journey to become members of Alpha Phi Alpha Fraternity, Inc., Beta Chapter during the winter and spring of 1993. Phil went on without us last year, having been able to more quickly balance the high demand of discipline required, and made the 1992 pledge line.

Pledging involved hours and hours of time after practice until the wee hours of the night. Each night, we were taught the facets of the fraternity system. We learned about every single member of the fraternity dating back twenty years. We learned about the founding members and the history. And most of all, we learned more about one another. The amount of time we spent together, the exhausting tasks we had to complete together, and the reliance we had to have on one another bonded us in a way we never anticipated.

Early in the process, the fresh pledgees began to look to me, Joey, and Brett for guidance. After all, we had gone through the pre-pledge process as sophomores even though our grades didn't allow us to complete it. Now that we were juniors, we had a year of knowledge, studying, and learning under our belts. Joey, Brett, and I were tighter than ever. Another junior named Steve gravitated to us pretty quickly and rounded out our inner circle. Steve was tall and dark chocolate. And he was a former runner, so his slender build added to the list of reasons the ladies swooned around him. I remembered Steve from the track interest meeting when we were freshmen. Although he ran in high school, he ultimately decided not to run at Howard. When we were reintroduced as potential pledgees for Alpha, we connected easily.

Steve also introduced me to his fellow New Jersey-bred comrade and runner, Ali. Ali was a freshman, but he came into Howard as a former All-American and was immediately a force on the track team. Ali couldn't begin the pledge process for Alpha because campus policy prohibited students from pledging their freshman year. However, he was a huge support for me while I was going through the process. Getting to know each other as teammates, I learned that we dealt with similar home issues, including a parent battling alcoholism. We leaned on each other and had many therapeutic and comforting late night discussions. We were both in the same situation; there was no returning home, and we were at Howard to finish with a degree for the promise of a future.

We both also struggled financially as college students and often found ways to supplement our meals at the university cafe by sneaking extra food. We would fill up containers of Tupperware for snacks and extra meals. One particular weekend, we did not successfully prepare and ran short on food. I will never forget it. Ali and I were walking down Georgia Avenue on the front side of Howard's campus. Somehow, our conversation diverted, and we began discussing how hungry we were. At that time, my pockets were empty, and Ali's were almost the same with the exception of a five-dollar bill.

He said, "All I have is five dollars, but we can split it."

And that is exactly what we did. We went to Yums Carry-Out and purchased a meal for $4.95. It was the best chicken wings and fries I had ever had! It was also the day I realized Ali was a true friend. As we used to say, he was a "ride or die." We were going to stick by each other, even during our lowest moments. It was a friendship that meant we would pull together during tough times, strengthening that bond further.

And the times were tough. One night after hours of tasks and time with the big brothers, Brett, Steve, another line brother of ours, Donnie Hoskey, and I staggered through the dark back alley to my dorm room in Cook Hall. We passed out from exhaustion, each of us finding space on my small twin bed to curl up and catch a few hours of sleep before we needed to get up for classes.

By seven o'clock, my alarm clock went off and startled me out of a deep REM sleep.

"Yo, wake up y'all." I tapped Brett. "Come on. Wake up." The guys started to wake, moving slowly at first, then quickly, realizing we had to make a move and get going to our classes.

"Man, I'm starving! Dez, you got any food? You know we can't be seen in the cafe," Brett said. It was a rule of our pledge process. You had to stay lowkey and could be seen on campus only in classes. He glanced around my tiny room and then took a few steps toward the mini-fridge.

I warned him before he opened it, "Ain't nothin' in there, dude."

Brett took a chance anyway and opened the door, hoping I was mistaken. Besides the couple of packets of ketchup and a half-empty bottle of Gatorade, it was empty.

Their eyes got bigger, their pupils dilated, and their mouths were wide open when I told them, "But I did move some of my meal plan money from the cafe and started an account at University Grill. I can call and order some break-fast if one of y'all can run over there and pick it up."

That became part of our routine for the rest of the pledge process. On the really late and challenging nights, my line brothers crashed in my room, and we all refueled with break-fast from University Grill.

I felt as if I was sleepwalking my way through school for those weeks. But we became mentally, emotionally, spiritu-ally, and physically stronger. We rarely perceived any of our confidential tasks as so difficult, as so challenging that we could not conquer them together. It was mind over matter most days, and we did the unthinkable to overcome all the odds and obstacles. And most of all, we learned to get out of our own way.

Finally, it was time for the death march, the last phase in our fraternal rites of passage process. It was a frigid February night. Temperatures hung around the mid-twenties most of the night. We stood in a line, one behind another. Each of us was given seven bricks—symbolic of the founding Jewels of our fraternity—connected by rope that we had to carry on our backs as we squatted in a crouched position. We didn't know at the time, but we would remain in that position for the duration of the walk up the campus hill to the main yard, which was just over a half mile. Each step was methodical and at a tedious pace, called out by one of the big brothers.

"Step!" We all moved in unison.

After several minutes, we heard, "Step!" And we all moved in unison again.

Again, several minutes went by, then, "Step!" And again, we all moved in unison.

I was one of the chosen ones. Because three of our line brothers could not carry their bricks for health reasons, I found myself with an extra pair to carry. Phil, my special big brother in the pledge process, would have no mercy on me and would demand I take every step with authority.

Two hours into the march, Big Brother Phil said, "Come on, Dez, you are more than halfway there now." It was a blow to my gut, but I soon began to picture myself in a familiar position: running for my teammates with half of the race to go, my legs burning and my chest ready to explode. Only now, it was my line brothers rather than my teammates who depended on me. I went to that place I had been before, elevating my consciousness above the physical pain. I had done this during workouts when my body said, *Stop*, but my mind fervently screamed, *Keep going.* I knew how to manage discomfort and pain. It was familiar to me.

So, I kept going. *Just keep going, Dez. Just don't stop.*

And we kept going.

"Step!" We all moved in unison.

Although my breath was visible in the cold air, sweat poured down my extremities. It was one of the most backbreaking and vigorous tasks I have endured. At some point during the last grueling hour, I don't remember feeling or hearing clearly. It was as if I had elevated to another plane and was beyond the point of reason.

And then, we were done. We completed the task. And now, I was officially a proud member of Alpha Phi Alpha Fraternity, Inc., Beta Chapter.

We pushed our physical and mental capacities beyond what we thought were our limits. We learned that a common struggle with a common goal can always lead to a common bond, one that we would have for a lifetime, beyond those glory days in undergraduate at Howard.

CHAPTER 13

LEANING AT THE FINISH LINE

I was now an Alpha man. I put my all into the process and was humbled to belong to a legacy of dynamic Black men who were leading their communities. Becoming an Alpha man was a journey that challenged me in ways that I never anticipated. And it was a dream come true. I entered my senior year with fresh confidence.

Finding balance wasn't easy, but eventually, I hit my stride with school, Alpha, and running. My senior year flew by, and I was having the time of my life. I didn't even get discouraged when my advisor informed me that I would not be able to graduate on time. I would have to take classes for a fifth year. It wasn't surprising because I switched majors a few times and failed miserably during my sophomore year. And strangely enough, I was actually relieved. I wanted the safety and security of the Mecca for another year.

During the fall of my fifth year, as a super senior, I elevated my training for cross country. This would be my last season as a college athlete. I began to train twice a day—one practice with the team and one on my own. My weekly mileage hovered around one hundred, and it was a full-time job. I wasn't just focused, I was fixated. I still felt as if I had something to prove and owed it to my coach, my team, and myself to take a top-ten finish at the Mid-Eastern Athletic Conference (MEAC) championships and garner all-conference honors this school year.

Coach Moultrie noticed my intensity and called me into his office after our first cross country practice that fall. He again sat behind that old, tattered desk with his hands behind his head, cowboy boots propped on top of it, and leaned back in his chair. "Son, I see you've done your homework!" he said with a slight smile. "You were a few seconds off our practice course record, so I can tell you came back this season ready to handle business."

"Thanks, Coach!" I said with a big, silly grin. Coach could tell I had trained hard over the summer, and at our practices, I began to lead the warmup routines, my teammates quickly followed my lead. I encouraged them, my positive attitude and leadership clearly stood out.

"If you're ready, I want you to be our captain this season. It hasn't been a smooth ride for you, but somehow, you're still here, and you're a man of your word. You've shown integrity and commitment, and I want you to lead our team. Think you can handle that?" Coach asked.

I nodded my head vigorously and blinked back the unexpected tears. After I cleared the lump in my throat, I replied, "I would be honored, Coach! Thank you for the opportunity. I won't let you down!" I felt so proud of myself. It wasn't easy, but I had found the strength to return to the team and earn back my scholarship. *And now captain?* This was a validation.

I shook my head in disbelief as I walked out of Coach's office with a delightful bounce in my step.

About six weeks later, it was clear I was having a fairytale fall cross country season. I managed to get beaten by only two runners the entire season, and I actually came back to beat one of them in a later meet. I kept my training at a high level and didn't build in any recovery phases so that I could train through most of the season.

With two weeks to go before the MEAC championships, I was ready to ease my rigorous training. That would allow my body to heal and refresh. Most coaches refer to this as the peaking or tapering phase of the season, which gives runners a mental and physical boost at the most important moment: championship time.

One day during practice, I took off from the starting line to run the "dip" loop at practice—the route had a big hill and dip midway through the course. I started the 3.5-mile loop with a slight cough that worsened as the run went on. Coach Moultrie also noticed I was coughing profusely. Once I returned from the quick loop, he gruffly said, "Desmond, that's it for you for the day. You need to rest and calm that cough."

I obliged and rushed to get a meal from the cafe, knocked out my reading for the night, and turned in early to grab an extra hour or two of sleep. I figured I needed a little rest.

The next morning, my cough worsened and was now accompanied by tightness and congestion in my chest. I tried to press on through classes and then tried an easy run later that day at practice, but it became unbearable. The coughing, phlegm, headache, and chest pains persisted. I grabbed some cough medicine on the way back to my dorm room and immediately gulped down a cup. Once I showered, I curled up and tucked in with several sheets and blankets for the night. I woke up in the wee hours of the night with sweat pouring down my cheeks and my forehead on fire. As I pulled off the blankets, I broke out in chills. I couldn't manage much more, so I threw on my sweats, bundled up, and staggered a few blocks to the Howard University Hospital emergency room.

Sitting there at three o'clock in the morning, I was in a daze despite all the patients around me being ushered in for treatment. After an hour, I was finally able to see a nurse, who took my vitals and confirmed my fever. Then I waited another two hours to see a doctor. After the doctor performed a series of checks and tests, he diagnosed me with bronchitis.

"Well, if you take the antibiotics, rest, and take care of yourself, you should be back in a couple weeks to full strength," the doctor said.

"Oh, no, but I have my championships in less than two weeks. Actually, they're in a week and four days, to be exact," I responded.

He replied, "There is no way I would recommend you do any running over the next two to three weeks. With the stress of running on your lungs, along with the cold air, it would be a recipe for disaster. Unfortunately, I think your season is over."

"What do you mean it's over?" I said as my eyes began to flood. "You just don't understand. My team needs me, and this is something I need to do. I'm the captain, and I just can't let them down! I just can't!"

He saw the look in my eyes and warned me with an increased sternness in his voice, "It would be dangerous for you to continue to run under these conditions."

He wrote me a prescription for antibiotics and gave me a sympathetic pat on the back. He knew his medical advice was a huge blow.

I slid off the table and walked down the hallway to the elevator. I left the hospital feeling more upset about the diagnosis and his declaration about my season being over than I did about the symptoms and discomfort. *How could this be happening again? It can't end this way!*

My senior year at Horace Mann ended with me limping across the finish line at the state meet because of a late season stress fracture in my foot. *And now,* I thought, *I won't even get a chance to compete in my last championship race as a collegiate runner?* I felt as if I had let my high school team down because I couldn't compete at full strength in our championships; now, it appeared I couldn't escape the same fate in college.

After getting my prescription filled and some more sleep that morning, I called Coach Moultrie to let him know I needed some time off. I didn't come completely clean, though. I simply said, "I think I have a bad cold."

With concern in his voice, he replied, "Rest up, Desmond. And get healthy before championships."

After a few days of antibiotics and rest, I was feeling better, and my coughing subsided. I was still weak but hopeful for a full recovery. By the end of the week, I was back out at practice, but I wasn't running. I was there for moral support and to cheer on my teammates. Many of them were concerned about me, but I played it cool. "It's just a bad cold," I assured them. "I'll be back stronger than ever for championships." But each time I coughed through my bundled scarf and coat, their looks of concern returned.

The Monday before the race, I joined the team for an easy three-mile run just to get my legs back under me and to test out my health. The run was so-so. My coughing was at a minimum and was bearable. As the team trotted more miles, I refrained from doing too much. I knew that in five days, I had to cover more mileage at a much faster pace. My training suggested that I could meet my desired time, but this easy run suggested otherwise.

As I was sitting at my desk later that night trying to stay on top of my academic work, I had a coughing spell that shook my confidence. My plan was to rest another day and then do an easy frolic run Wednesday to be ready for the course preview on Friday. Midway through the season, I grew more confident that I could place in the top three at the conference championships. Now the plan was to do whatever it took for top ten and All-MEAC honors. I wanted to give my team the best shot to score as well as possible.

On the Wednesday before the meet, there was no major change in my condition during a five-mile run, so I believed I could muster the energy and effort to endure discomfort for the sake of the team. I chose not to run the course Friday after arriving at the meet location, the day before the race. I walked a portion of it to get familiar with the gentle rolling hills and intricacies of the course.

It was finally race day, and I found myself repeating stanzas of the poem that inspired me the most, *Invictus* by William Earnest Henley. My self-talk continued. *I can do this. My thousands and thousands of miles will pay off. The team needs me.*

As I warmed up, the struggle began to take over. Coach Moultrie noticed and pulled me off to the side.

"Desmond, are you sure you're okay to run?" he questioned. I looked at him, but before I could answer, he knew by the look in my eyes that there was no turning back for me. He put his hand on my shoulder and said, "You're one of the tough ones. They don't make them like they used to." He gave my back a sturdy pat and said, "Let's go, son!"

Despite my conservative warmup, I jogged back to my teammates with a pep in my step. I checked in with my teammates and gave them a final rally as we all headed to the starting line.

"Come on, guys. This is it! We've trained for this," I said as I patted a couple of the guys next to me on the back. I didn't feel great, but I knew I needed to set the tone for my team. "No one out-guts us out there! Now, let's go! Bison on three!"

My heart was beating through my chest from the adrenaline. This is the moment I had prepared for—a chance for redemption from my senior year of high school.

"Runners, set!" *Bang!* went the starter's gun. We stampeded from the starting line. I intentionally found a relaxed and comfortable initial pace, pumping my arms in a cadence in sync with my strides. I wanted to make sure I was in the position to strike in the second half of the race. After the first mile, I was pleased to find myself on the back end of the lead pack in around tenth place. Mile two began to take a toll. Every few steps were accompanied with a cough or two. By mile three, I was praying for God to put me out of my misery. My chest felt as if it was being smashed by a sledgehammer with each breath. My throat burned. I forced my mind to recite the *Invictus* lines that matched my unbowed desire for winning and continued to push on.

Physically struggling and heartbroken with two miles to go, I was holding on for dear life. I found myself in familiar territory again. It resembled the asthma attack I suffered in my first year of high school. I struggled, but somehow, I finished. I survived that. I survived the death march. I survived the perils of Gary. I was a survivor. Even when unsure how, I willed myself to persevere.

I climbed into fifth place and was running alongside teammate Damion Rowe, but I didn't stay there long. I began to fade.

"Come on, Desmond!" Coach Moultrie kept yelling from the sideline for me to hold on. He knew I was in agony, and I did not look at full strength.

In the last mile, I continued to lose my rhythm and my cadence slowed. With each step, I coughed. I labored to breathe. No matter how much air I tried to muster, my pathways only allowed in slithers of oxygen. I faded to twelfth, then thirteenth, then fourteenth, then fifteenth place. With less than a half mile to go, I began to stagger and desperately reach for the finish line. It was the longest 600 meters of my life. Now in sixteenth place and with 400 meters to go, I pushed on all cylinders. My vision became blurry, my legs felt like two steel rods, my head felt as if it had cannons firing, one after another.

With each step, I staggered side to side, following the encouraging voices to the finish line, unable to see clearly. Minutes later, I woke up in the back of an ambulance with an intravenous (IV) drip and an oxygen mask. I was exhausted and distraught. I heard Coach Moultrie giving orders.

"Go ahead and take him to the nearest hospital. I'll meet him there." I somehow gained enough composure to deny the transport.

"No, no hospital. What place? What place?" I was discombobulated, but I needed to know how I finished. *Was I able to hold on enough for the team?*

"Desmond, have you been sick?" one of the medics asked.

Not thinking clearly, I didn't realize what I was saying until it was too late.

I mumbled with all my energy, "Bronchitis. I have bronchitis."

Coach's eyes widened as he realized exactly what I was dealing with. He stood anxiously watching as the medical team replaced the empty bag of fluids and quickly administered a second bag. I lay limply on the table under the medical tent, my head spinning, and incredible pressure on my chest. After the medics emptied two bags of intravenous fluids, my condition improved.

Another medic told me that in addition to the potential of my bronchitis getting worse, I was also dehydrated, which added more stress to my body.

"Desmond, please take your antibiotics, drink plenty of fluids, and most of all, get some rest. You can seriously make your bronchitis much more severe." At that point, I was at the medics' mercy and fully willing to comply.

I eventually gained enough strength to sit up and crawl off the table. I stabilized myself on my feet and walked back to the bus with Coach Moultrie. Needless to say, it was a very awkward walk. He was upset I hadn't been transparent about my condition, but at the same time, he understood why I chose not to. I was more concerned about letting down the team. It brought me comfort when he revealed we would have performed far worse if I hadn't run.

On the ride home, I noticed that my cough had changed and now had a disgusting aftertaste. Upon returning to DC, I made another trudge to the emergency room and found myself with the same doctor who gave me the initial diagnosis. Already feeling like crap, I recounted the last week and a half to him and admitted I had disregarded his medical advice. He wasn't pleased. After running a series of tests, he came back with the news.

"Unfortunately, your bronchitis has developed into pneumonia, and we will need to admit you at least overnight."

This time I was willing to oblige, willing to do anything to get rid of the cough, the phlegm, the fever, and the chills.

Weeks later I lay on my bed reflecting on the race. While upset with my dismal nineteenth-place finish, I was comforted knowing I stood with my brothers, my teammates. I had gone to war with them, in desperate circumstances. Many of my teammates told me how insane I was to have run in that condition, but I could not live with the regret of not attempting to run at all.

CHAPTER 14

FROM PLEDGING TO PURPOSE

My fifth year in undergrad continued my evolution into a leader. While finishing up my courses for my exercise physiology major and allied sciences minor—the degree path I eventually landed on, eventually leading me to pursue medical school—I followed in Charles Graham's footsteps and was elected as the president of Alpha Phi Alpha Fraternity, Inc., Beta Chapter. In turn, I planned programs that impacted the young fellas coming in as freshmen. I led service projects, began a tutorial and mentorship program for elementary school children, and managed a dormitory as a resident assistant.

I bonded with my fraternity brothers in a way that connected us for a lifetime, a major part of that journey being the time we spent in step practice.

Brett was our step master, who choreographed the steps, demanded our best, and kept us motivated when we practiced into the wee hours of the night after a long day of classes. As a step team, we designed and practiced our routines each night for weeks on end, then performed all over the country at shows where we typically won and earned prize money to donate to causes our fraternity supported.

One evening in early September, my big brother, Connie Williams, called me up with an idea that I couldn't pass up.

"Dez, I need bros to support this cause. I've spent some time in South Africa, and it has been life changing." I could hear the passion and sincerity in Connie's voice. "I want to start something where bros go to Soweto and teach stepping," he continued. "There are people there that will teach traditional Gumboot dancing to bros. What I'm talking about is a cultural exchange. I'm calling the program 'Step Afrika!'"

As Connie talked, I grew more and more excited. "Yo, bro, that sounds amazing. When would we go? How much does it cost us? What do you need me to do?" I asked.

"Well, we need to work out the finances, but it won't be cheap. We need to go during the winter break when bros are off from school," Connie started. "It would be work, man. Every day, bros would need to be ready to teach stepping to the kids and to learn the South African dances in exchange," Connie explained.

At our next fraternity chapter meeting, I introduced the idea to the other brothers, and they immediately agreed to support the project in South Africa. We spent the next three months fundraising—competing in step shows to win prize money, hosting social events on campus, and asking our families and friends for donations. We each had to raise $1,500. As college students, the goal seemed nearly unachievable, but we were fully determined to make it happen.

By early December, we had reached our goal. There were ten of us set to take the trip across the Atlantic, along with Connie and two of Connie's friends from Howard who worked for one of the organizations that our fundraising supported. The organization's mission was to help feed children in need in Johannesburg.

"Dez, I don't know how y'all did it, but this is amazing," Connie said to me as we walked through Washington National Airport on our way to the terminal for our first flight to John F. Kennedy Airport in New York before switching planes for our sixteen-hour direct flight to Johannesburg, South Africa. *I can't believe I'm about to fly to Africa. Africa!* It felt surreal. I still felt like just a regular kid from Gary. *And now I'm about to go international? This is crazy.*

The past few months, I hustled the best way I knew how, with intense focus that neared obsession. In one way, it felt as if I had crossed the finish line with my hands raised high in the air, but in another way, I was at the starting line about to begin the most important race of my life.

Eighteen-plus hours later, we landed in the motherland. I was exhausted, but I was too excited to succumb to the tiredness. I was grateful to feel this type of anticipation, especially after the tough days and weeks since the cross country championships didn't live up to my expectations. Not showing up for my teammates in the way I had hoped was weighing me down mentally and emotionally at my core. And now, the thing that had been central to my identity for so much of my life was a thing of the past. My running career was over. *What do I do without running? Who am I without a team to run with?* With my head spinning, it was refreshing to have a change of scenery.

We loaded into a van and headed to our host homes in Yeoville, an artsy, creative suburb of Johannesburg. It had commercial areas, tall skyscrapers, and highways that resembled a bustling metropolis. I hadn't expected to see much modernization. Like so many other Americans, I had misconceptions and held stereotypes about Africa. I thought everyone would be walking around in kente cloth. I imagined grasslands and dirt roads. Within minutes, my entire perception of my original homeland was disrupted.

We met our host families and settled in. Brett and Kevin Thompson—who were also on a five-year special plan—and I stayed together in a quaint bungalow-style house with a host family affiliated with the Soweto Dance Company. The family was incredibly warm and accommodating, embracing us in hugs as we entered their home and immediately asking whether we were hungry or just needed rest.

The next day, we rejoined our other fraternity brothers and climbed back into the van to begin our trek into Soweto. We would spend most of our days on this trip at one of the community centers, exchanging and representing our cultures through dance and dialogue.

As we got closer to the town of Soweto, our surroundings began to drastically change. Rows and rows of shanties appeared, small structures made with sheets of tin nailed together. The homes made my former 500-square-foot apartment in Westbrook Apartment Complex look like a mansion. There was no running water and limited electricity. Soweto Townships are South Africa's largest urban complex. It grew out of the shantytowns and slums that arose with the arrival of Black laborers from rural areas, in particular between the two World Wars. (History, 2020) The main streets were dirt roads. Apartheid had ended a year ago, yet its remnants still rang through the neighborhoods of the township.

Although apartheid was supposedly designed to allow different races to develop on their own, the system placed White South Africans in power to assume wealth and forced Black South Africans into poverty and desolation. (History, 2020)

Observing the streets of Soweto, it hit me. I saw kids who looked like me who never had an opportunity to run, race, and compete the way that I did. I was letting my disappointment about my final race linger, leaving me mildly depressed. I was looking at my final moments on the cross country course as a representation of who I was, when, in fact, I had gained so much from my running. I had formed new friendships, I had gained another mentor in my coach, and I had developed as a leader and role model. I was humbled and embarrassed to realize that many issues more significant than my bruised ego existed in the world.

We arrived at the community center, a large open structure with indoor and outdoor rooms. It had been built in the past year and looked out of place among the shanties and dirt roads. People milled around the community center, the roads busy with people walking, having conversations, or accomplishing chores near their tiny homes. When I stepped out of the van into the warm sunlight, it did not matter that I was surrounded by such extreme poverty. As my feet touched the ground and I surveyed the faces of the people, I was *home*. I felt *home*. I felt belonging and warmth and energy and light and love. I was surprised by the lively spirit of community. I didn't know any of the people outside of my fraternity brothers in the van, but I felt safe and seen and connected.

As I surveyed my surroundings, I took a deep breath. It was one of the most humbling moments of my life. We gathered inside the new but modest community center and met the performers and dancers who were part of the Soweto Dance Company. Jackie was the coordinator. He was a lean and laidback guy with an easy smile who appeared to be in his mid-twenties. Together, our two groups—the dance company and our fraternity—would host a two-week cultural exchange program for the children in Soweto, teaching during the week and venturing out beyond the township and Johannesburg during the weekend.

The children arrived within the hour, and we prepared to start our first session. There were about sixty children that first day, ages ranging from about six years old to seventeen. They were energetic, friendly, eager, welcoming, and curious. But most of all, loving. You could feel how appreciative they were to be with us, to learn something American from people who looked like them. Their humility was magnetic.

As I stood in front of the large group, butterflies invaded my belly, and adrenaline got my heart pumping. I had stepped in front of thousands of people before, but this was different. I felt honored to be in front of these children, and for some reason, I desperately wanted their approval. I wanted validation of my kinship.

"Helloooo! I'm Dez, and these are my brothers," I began in an elevated voice. "We are Alpha Phi Alpha! Repeat that for me. Say 'Alpha Phi Alpha!'"

They said it back in unison. "Alpha Phi Alpha!" Their smiles and bright eyes encouraged me as I continued.

"You can be louder than that. Say 'Alpha Phi Alpha!'" I yelled with more volume than the first time.

"Alpha Phi Alpha!" they all yelled back.

"Yeah! That's more like it. We're here to teach you something called stepping. You will need your voice, just like that! First, we're going to show you what it looks like. Who wants to see me and my brothers step for you?"

The group cheered for us. "Me!" several shouted, jumping up and down. "Yes!" some yelled. "Me, me, me!"

The rest of my fraternity brothers joined me in front of the crowd, and within seconds, we had them enthralled. Our stomping and clapping and chanting in unison was familiar yet beautifully unique to them. Once we finished our routine, the crowd of children and teenagers erupted in applause. We had them hooked, eager to learn how to feel the percussive and rhythmic moves.

The next few hours flew by. We exchanged stepping and dance movements, sure. But we also exchanged appreciation and affirmation as people from the diaspora with different experiences yet common struggles. Our spirits recognized that commonality, and the connection was palpable.

During our lunch break, I sauntered through the streets nearby with my fraternity brothers, trying to take it in. We were ambassadors of our fraternity, of Howard University, and of the United States. We were on a sixteen-day cultural exchange program in South Africa, just one year after apartheid ended. Nelson Mandela was the president. I had seen bits and pieces of South Africa's recent events unfold on the news, and now here I was, right smack in the middle of the country.

We walked and talked and greeted people who smiled and waved. I began to reflect on the similarities of the Black experience in South Africa and in America. If I squinted just a bit, I almost felt like I was home. The same warmth and connection to the people. And the same reminders of poverty and marginalization.

Areas of the United States were still struggling from four hundred years of enslavement and the systematic racist policies of that period, but seeing this devastation on another continent was overwhelming. Most of the people we saw had very little. Some of the children were malnourished, had psychological issues, and were maladjusted. I saw an entire community of people who were left to fend for themselves, living in inhumane conditions with few resources. My heart ached seeing it plainly in front of me.

After our first week, we left the city and ventured to the rural area outside of Soweto Townships. This time, we stayed with families whose homes had cracks in the tin roofs, often allowing water and rubbish to fall on their dirt and rock floors. When I asked to use the restroom, I was directed about 200 feet away to the communal toilets. My stomach could not handle the conditions of the toilets, and my lunch found a new home on the side of the road. *Can the world be this cruel? Can people be this cruel? Where is humanity?* I had so much gratitude and guilt gnawing at my soul. Gratitude and guilt tugging at me, knowing I could have been born anywhere in the world, with any parents, in any given situation. I grew more grateful for the sacrifices my mom had always made for me and my sister, and unexpectedly, I traded a bit of the anger I harbored for my dad with appreciation for his imperfect love for me. Somehow, my problems were no longer that important.

I knew I needed to run again. I was resentful, depressed, and bitter that my college running career ended the way that it did. And I hadn't run for months after. Running was always my sanctuary, my outlet. But I had allowed a wall to build, and I hid behind it, wallowing in my misery. After being in South Africa, learning what I did, experiencing the people like I did, that wall started to crumble, and I again yearned for the feeling of being within myself. I laced up my sneakers one early morning before we were due back in Soweto and ventured out into the neighborhoods for an easy run. It was the first time I ran just for the sheer goodness of running—no meet to prepare for, no mileage to calculate. Just freely being with myself.

A few days before our departure, my fraternity brothers and I took part in a community festival, a day-long block party that stretched for miles. There was a parade, singing, and dancing. Performers displayed their talents on the big stage. Delicious food was cooking at every turn. Everyone in great spirits. We danced and danced and stepped and partied. It was a celebration of freedom. The beauty and richness of this moment belied the oppression and marginalization that had been forced on Black South Africans.

That day marked one year since apartheid ended and Mandela was released and elected president. Mandela was unrightfully arrested in 1962 and received a life sentence two years later. He spent twenty-seven years in prison as a result of fighting for freedom, equality, truth, peace, and love for all mankind. The irony and injustice of apartheid was that Blacks were the majority in the country, yet were dominated politically, socially, and economically by the nation's minority White population from 1948 to 1994. (History, 2020) My fraternity brothers and I heard stories from some of the South Africans we met throughout our visit, detailing how they were treated and how they were denied the right to vote. We learned that anyone who opposed apartheid during that time risked being tortured, punished, or subjected to an unfair trial.

Over the course of nearly two weeks, my appreciation for where I came from, for what my kinsman had gone through, grew exponentially. I would not go back to the United States as the same man.

On our last morning with our primary host family back in Johannesburg, they cooked us a farewell breakfast. Because I had seen the sacrifices and hardships up close, I knew that hosting us for nearly two weeks was not easy financially. I was humbled by the family's gestures to ensure we were comfortable and that our accommodations were pleasing. So, when a plate full of eggs was placed in front of me, I knew I could not turn it down. To do so would have been an ultimate disrespect to the family. I couldn't tell them that eggs physically make me sick. I knew it was customary to show your appreciation by eating the food prepared for you, so I started to panic.

I leaned over to Brett and Kevin, whispering, "I can't eat these eggs; I'm allergic." Brett quickly scooped a third of them off of my plate and so did Kevin, but I had to suck it up to inhale the rest. I became more nauseated with each spoonful, but I cleaned my plate.

I masked my discomfort from our host family, smiling and thanking them for such a wonderful breakfast. There was no way I could be transparent about how I was feeling, knowing they had sacrificed to open their home to us and ensured we had such a wonderful, life-changing experience.

On our final evening, we headed toward downtown Yeoville to experience more of the culture of the city. We approached a nightclub and saw the line wrapped around the block. But our host from the Soweto Dance Company waved us along, and we were escorted through the short line meant for all the VIP guests. We piled into the basement of a sleek and quaint hole in the wall. The club was warm, to say the least, and filled with smoke and vibrant people. We sat there drinking, talking, and laughing while we listened to several jazz artists.

Later in the evening, we noticed a small commotion as a trumpeter entered the stage. The crowd began to buzz and then roared. He stood still and waited for the right moment, the moment when the crowd paused in expectation. *Who is this guy? Whoever he is, they love him here,* I thought. He brought his trumpet to his lips, closed his eyes and took us on a journey. We were captivated by his very first note.

His syncopated rhythmic patterns silenced the crowd. Then he passionately sang, "Apartheid!" The tune of his trumpet, along with his ability to tell the story of the angry coal workers, took me to a place that made me feel like I was on the train with them that night. I was with the men forcibly removed from their loved ones and forced to work in mines. These men were transported away from their families and worked sixteen hours or more a day for almost no pay. The trumpeter's voice rang out over the crowd as he sang about the depths of pain and the literal depths of the coal mines where Black South Africans worked under treacherous conditions. In the pit of my stomach, I could feel the agony in the belly of the earth as he played.

This musical performance put a spotlight on the centuries of exploitation faced by Black South Africans. To gain economic and political power, White South Africans destroyed families and devastated communities. I knew what it felt like to be a product of these evils; his lyrics touched my soul and stirred my spirit in anguish.

I left the nightclub with chills in my body and tears in my eyes, moved and transformed. I attribute those feelings to the famous jazz trumpeter Hugh Masekela and his trademark song, "Stimela." His words and notes pierced through generations of pain to comfort and console a nation of people gathered in that tiny nightclub. That night, I recognized the depth of history and connection shared by my current and historical homelands. That night, I recognized—no I *felt*—where I came from and who I really was.

PART III

COACHING

"The eagle does not escape the storm;
it simply uses the storm to lift it higher.
In fact, it rises on the very winds that
bring the storm."

—*LOIS EVANS*

CHAPTER 15

COMMUNITY AND CALLING

———

After that life-altering experience with Step Afrika! in South Africa, I was determined to buckle down on my academics in my last semester at Howard. I needed to do well in my courses to accomplish my post-graduation goals.

Months away from graduating, I knew I had a big grind ahead—a hefty course load of eighteen credit hours, equating to six classes, and my dream of medical school. I was fascinated by the human body's ability to accept and adapt to challenges, depending on which systems were being stressed. Running in college, I learned how to create and manipulate workouts to reach my optimal performance in everything from the 800 meters to the 10,000 meters. While Coach Moultrie was an exceptional role model, leader, and supporter, distance running was not his specialty. I was often left to my own devices when training. Having to take on such a huge role in developing my personalized workouts became an invaluable skill and important experience in my coaching career.

Despite my subpar performance at our MEAC Championships, Coach Moultrie named me team most valuable runner and even named the 4x800-meter relay event in my honor at the annual Howard Relays track meet.

Sitting in Coach's office that spring, chit-chatting about my post-graduation plans, he said something that stuck with me: "Desmond, you're a special kid. Many guys wouldn't have finished what they started and definitely wouldn't have toed the line with your illness at championships. You have the true Olympic spirit and work ethic. It was a pleasure to have you in the program, son."

I left his office overwhelmed. I was never the most talented on any of my teams, but I was always recognized for working hard and being very coachable. I appreciated coaches with a competitive spirit but who also knew where to draw the line. They didn't ruin the positive experience or opportunity sports could provide for people who worked hard, stayed committed and acted as team players. As the last coach who would ever train me as a runner, Coach Moultrie affirmed who I would become as a result of running.

With a new pep in my step, I set my sights on finishing undergrad and figuring out which graduate school program would put me in the best position to take the MCAT and pursue medical school.

On a beautiful day in May, my graduation came and went in a blur. Besides Howard's renowned homecoming in the fall, graduation was the most exciting time on campus. You could sense the jubilation from the family members and friends assembled to celebrate. My grades had been strong during my last three semesters—just strong enough to push my cumulative GPA over the threshold to graduate with honors.

My mom, aunt, and sister cheered when my name was called, instantly prompting me to break into a refulgent smile as I waved toward them in the crowd. We celebrated all weekend, and I cherished knowing I made my family proud, especially my mom. She had sacrificed so much. She had been constantly disappointed and let down by my dad, and she finally had her own piece of happiness. I was honored that one of my achievements made her light up.

My dad was there, too, posing for pictures with me in my royal blue cap and gown. I knew he was proud, and I remember him saying those words to me. However, by that point, I had convinced myself that it didn't matter. I graduated without his support. Five years of college, and he never gave me meaningful advice, real words of encouragement, or financial assistance. I was so conflicted about our relationship. I had become a man despite him, without having genuine conversations of substance and without really getting to know him or much about his life.

* * *

"I put the agenda together and also printed out sign-up sheets," Jami Harris said as she handed me a manila folder.

"Oh, wow. Okay, thanks," I said with slight surprise. Jami once again took the initiative to organize our team. Although I had met her only recently, she had already become a dedicated volunteer.

"Well, let's write down the schedule so folks can decide which tutoring shifts they want to take," I continued.

"There are copies of the schedule in the folder, too," Jami said with a smirk. She was already anticipating the logistics and organization I needed. I was in my second year of graduate school at Howard with a lot on my plate, juggling courses to meet my medical school prerequisites, running a tutoring and mentoring program I started called Each One Teach One, and working as a graduate assistant in one of the dorms. I needed all the help I could get. I chose to pursue my graduate studies in nutritional sciences, which complimented my exercise physiology background. I had a heavy load, but I finally felt like I was hitting my stride.

In my first year as a resident assistant during my junior year, I had begun tutoring at Gage Eckington Elementary School, just a block from Howard's campus. Some of my residents and I tutored the students a few days a week and enjoyed getting to know the kids and the principal, Ms. Brown. The school made me feel as if I was doing more than just volunteering my time. I was part of a community—a community for kids who were like me. The kids' infectious energy inspired me to be someone they looked up to. I had my community growing up in Gary. Imperfect as it was, it was my village. And now, Howard and DC were becoming my new village. I needed that connection to thrive, and I knew the kids needed it, too.

The next year, the school's funding was cut significantly, and principal Brown did not have the money to staff foreign language and music teachers. Of course, she also didn't have extra funding to hire tutors. So, I started Each One Teach One and began a formal relationship between Howard University students and her school.

Each One Teach One gained momentum on campus, and I had recruited a strong group of volunteers by the fall of my second graduate year. Our meetings were growing and a few of the volunteers stepped up to be leaders, including

Jami. She showed the same dedication and passion as I did for making a difference in the community.

Eventually, I began to operate Each One Teach One within the Howard University Student Association (HUSA) after I became the community service director for the organization. With help from other college students in my dorm, in my fraternity, and on the track team, I organized haunted houses, holiday parties, and field trips to Howard football and basketball games.

The Howard community fostered my bloom into a leader, and I embraced the responsibility the job demanded. I wanted to be the type of role model for others that Charles Graham had been for me. I even tried to look the part, strolling around campus with a briefcase!

"So tonight, we need to be sure that everyone knows what a serious commitment this is. We have to stress that, although they are volunteering, everyone has to be reliable and show up for their scheduled sessions on time with the kids. Principal Brown is depending on us," I urged Jami and the other lead volunteers organizing the program with me during our team meeting.

Jami chimed in with a question: "Desmond, do we have a system for covering the classes if someone gets sick? Maybe we should use a buddy system and schedule for alternates? That way we never have to depend on one person."

"That makes sense," I replied.

"Okay, cool. I put two slots for each shift on the sign-up sheets just in case," Jami said, smiling again.

"Always thinking ahead. I love it," I said, reciprocating the smile. I didn't say it then, but I was also thinking: *Man, she's smart, beautiful, and really cares about the kids, too. We make a good team.*

Over fifty volunteers showed up for our first meeting of the school year early that September. Within two weeks, nearly one hundred students signed up to be tutors and mentors. Jami became the director of operations for the program, and we began to spend more time together. In our symbiotic relationship, I kept dreaming up the big ideas to help the kids at Gage-Eckington, and she thought through all the practical details.

Jami originally volunteered to teach Spanish to kids at Gage, sparking the start of real conversations between us. She was petite, with long dark hair and an athletic build. Within a few weeks of working together, I began to look forward to her bright smile and easy laugh, and her reliability and organization helped propel Each One Teach One forward. We began to talk daily, meeting up midday in the HUSA office to check in on upcoming events at Gage or to plan the next volunteer meeting. She and her group of friends were fun and down-to-earth, and it sure made my life easier to have her around to help with the planning and organization of all our community service projects.

That November, we were hanging out in the HUSA office, and Jami asked, "Are you coming to the game tonight?"

"The basketball game? Naw, I probably don't have time. Plus, it's early in the season, so I'll wait until the games get a little more exciting," I said with a chuckle.

"You should come to the game to see me cheer," she said with a smile and slight head tilt.

"Wait, I thought you played soccer?" I asked.

"I do. Our season is in the fall, so we just played our last game a couple weeks ago. In the winter I cheer for men's basketball. It's fun. You should think about coming," she said as she got up from her seat. "See ya. Gotta run to class!"

"Later," I said as my eyes followed her out of the small office. *What is it about this girl?* She was still in undergrad, so there was a five-year age gap between us, but we connected well, and she was easy to talk to. She was an athlete and understood my passion for competing. We enjoyed swapping sports stories, and she was into the NFL and NBA as much as I was. She was also a serious student. She was an avid reader, and although I wasn't, I liked how excited she got when she told me about a book she was into. Maybe it was because she was from the Midwest, too, but there was an ease to our conversation and a light to her energy that drew me in. I shook my head and refocused on the notes from my last meeting with Principal Brown. We had a big holiday party to plan for the kids, and I needed to call a few more places to get toys and books donated.

I decided to go to that basketball game and a few others that winter. Jami and I became good friends, and we continued to increase the volume of community service programs within Each One Teach One. We recruited volunteers to assist at a local food shelter and organized food and clothing drives. We organized cleaning and revitalizations at schools and community centers. We led Big Brothers Big Sisters field trips to local museums and city landmarks. It felt as if we were really making a difference when we heard the joy around us, as if we were part of something bigger than us.

By early spring, I again got a strong feeling of purpose and passion when I started volunteering as a track and field coach at St. Gabriel's Catholic School, just a couple of miles from Howard. By the time I left my first practice at St. Gabriel's, I was hooked. It was so natural. By the end of the second practice, I knew every kid's name and we had come up with our own chant. Leaving practice that day, I remember thinking,

Man, I love this! Coaching is so much fun, and time flies when I'm at practice.

Within weeks, the kids were all bought in. They came to practice ready to work out. I did my best to make it fun, to connect with each kid, to get to know their interests, and to encourage them throughout the practice. But most of all, I wanted to emulate the lasting impression my two dynamic coaches left on me when it came to the power of relationships, team culture, and leadership. By this time, my relationship with Jami had blossomed into a deep friendship. By spring break, I became the shoulder she cried on when things were on the rocks with her boyfriend. She was ready to call it off, and based on what she told me, I didn't like how he treated her either.

One day we sat outside Burr Gymnasium as Jami cried about something she learned about him. She knew she had to face the inevitable, but she still kept holding on for some reason.

"I can't believe him! I'm just so upset! How could he?" she continued to vent and cry as I sat and listened. During my undergrad days, I was one of those guys who didn't value relationships the way I should have and probably caused similar tears from a few of my ex-girlfriends. I had my share of fun dating, but I also made some mistakes I wasn't proud of.

"I don't know what to do. I thought I could trust him!" She used the back of her hand to wipe away the fresh set of tears that slid down her cheeks. I wanted to help, but I knew I couldn't give her any advice. She had to make this decision on her own.

When she took a breath, I said, "Come on. I have a few places I need to stop by on campus. Walk with me. It'll take your mind off things."

She took a deep sigh. "Okay. I guess so." She stood up, and I gave her a hug.

"It's going to be okay," I said as reassuringly as I could. She deserved better, but I kept my peace about it. I valued our friendship and didn't want to upset her more by telling her what she already knew deep down. We took our time, strolling and talking, and within a matter of minutes, she was smiling at one of my corny jokes.

It just felt natural when we were together. I then decided to take a leap of faith.

"Are you hungry?" I asked her after we finished my last errand.

Jami replied, "Yeah, a bit I guess."

"Let's go to Ben's Chili Bowl. The food is great. And the spot is historic. All kinds of celebrities and politicians have eaten there. It's a real chill place though."

She gave me a tiny smile and replied, "Okay. Sure, I'll go." A slight shift flashed in her eyes. I could tell she still wanted my company. And that was our turning point. It was our first unofficial date.

As I finished up graduate classes by mid-May, I began preparing to start a year-long post-baccalaureate program at Indiana University-Purdue University Indianapolis (IUPUI) before attending medical school. I embraced the idea of a gap year in order to take more health-related classes and participate in experiences that would enhance my chances of being admitted to medical school.

I had spent the previous summer on IUPUI's campus doing biomedical research with Edward T. Mannix as a result of advice from my pediatrician and mentor, Dr. Steve Simpson. While on campus, I was introduced to members of the medical admissions team. They were impressed with my work, and I finally achieved the necessary admission scores on my third attempt at the medical college admissions test (MCAT) after taking a Princeton Review course.

The Princeton Review introduced me to a different world, one that showed me what access meant. I had struggled on the first two attempts at the MCAT, as I did with my high school SAT, but when my aunt Beverly, my mom's youngest sister, suggested the course and volunteered to pay the $1,200 fee, a new door opened. I was determined to walk through that door so I could become a doctor. My aunt's generosity was an attempt to level the playing field for me. To this day, I am humbled my aunt recognized my potential and made it her business to ensure I had access.

My preparation was meticulous, the strategies made sense, and my endurance built up to a marathon level. Studying required an intensity that hearkened back to my early days as a runner. I doubled my study hours. I took flashcards and reading material with me everywhere and reviewed them at any free minute. It was like the MCAT was my championship meet, and I developed a training program for myself to peak at the right time. *Come on, Dez, you got this. Don't panic, stay relaxed, take three deep breaths, and dig deeper.* I passed on parties and social events. But I took the time to go on a run almost every day, which always made me feel more energized and less stressed.

I would certainly need that endurance during my final try at the MCAT. As we all sat in an overheated room on Howard's campus, delays extended the eight-hour test to ten and a half hours. I didn't fret. *Pain is temporary. Pride is forever. If you give up, you will never forgive yourself, and that pain will live forever.* The positive self-talk I learned as a runner paid off.

On the August weekend of the post-baccalaureate orientation at IUPUI, Jami rode to Baltimore-Washington International Airport with me. By this time, Jami and I were more than just friends. She had finally cut ties with the guy she was crying on my shoulder about earlier in the spring. She (and I) never looked back. We spent most days together that summer, enjoying the sights of the city. We would have long talks about everything. We had built a strong friendship during the past year, volunteering and working together with the kids at Gage. With each community service project, we fortified our bond and grew to depend on one another. We shared a passion for serving youth, and that mutual interest developed into a mutual attraction. At this point, we were finishing each other's sentences. Our connection was undeniable.

"I requested a transfer application yesterday," she said on the ride. "IUPUI has all the classes I need, so I don't think I'll need to switch my major."

We had already discussed how we could continue our relationship once I started the post-baccalaureate program in the fall. I wanted her close as I entered this next phase, but I knew it would be a huge sacrifice for her. I also knew I needed to stay focused on my goal of becoming a doctor. I was doing all the right things to get there. But I couldn't shake the uneasiness in my stomach on the car ride. *Am I making the right decision moving back to Indiana? Why am I not excited? I'm one step closer to my dream, right?*

As we were about to take the exit for the airport off Interstate 95, I felt my beige Isuzu Rodeo jerk, then sputter.

"What the heck?" I asked out loud. I looked over at Jami in the passenger seat.

She looked back at me, worried. "Whoa!" she said as the truck jerked again and began to decelerate.

In less than a minute, the truck completely stopped. I pulled it over to the shoulder before it conked out.

This has got to be a sign. For some reason, I was not meant to go to that post-baccalaureate orientation. My truck stopped and confirmed what I already knew. I didn't want to go. I never made it to the airport. Looking back, I know for sure that God stopped my plans. I didn't know what was next, but I knew I wasn't quite ready to be apart from Jami, from DC or from coaching.

CHAPTER 16

ROOKIE COACH

——

"Fella, I just want you to be happy and to be the best at whatever you decide to do," my mom said lovingly through the phone. It was winter 1997, and I was four months into teaching physical science at Archbishop Carroll High School in Washington, DC, just about two miles from Howard University. I looked forward to each day with my ninth and tenth grade students.

Teaching in my gap year, after deferring my post-baccalaureate program for a year, allowed me to combine my passions for kids, science, and service. Science challenged me intellectually, so diving into it every day with my students gave me joy. Plus, I was able to coach the cross country team at Carroll. When I made that solemn call to my mother, I was at a crossroads.

"Ma, I'm just not feeling excited about med school anymore. I really love what I'm doing. I'm not making any money, but I'm so happy teaching and coaching," I explained, my voice shifting slightly to a more jovial tone. I knew I didn't need it, but when she gave her approval, the relief was instant.

It was around this time that I also knew I wanted a future with Jami. We were spending nearly every day together, and we began to plan for our lives together. Our first Christmas was coming up, and although we wouldn't be together in person, that day, I had never been so meticulous about choosing gifts for someone. I wanted her to know how special she had become to me.

After the holidays, there was no turning back. Jami came to Gary, and I showed her my old high school and the places I told her about in my Gary stories. We drove to the different running trails, recreating the runs Chief challenged my team with. I took her to try the meals I craved at my favorite childhood spots. I needed Jami to really see who I was and where I came from. The man she met at Howard was a far cry from the boy I was in Gary. Regardless of the pollution, Gary was still my breath of fresh air, and I was very protective of my hometown. She needed to see my roots. And I needed to see whether she could connect to my family and my original community.

During that visit, Jami seemed comfortable around my family—Mama Hattie, Aunt Shirley, Shnicks, and definitely my mom. She showed a genuine interest in them all, asking questions about my childhood and listening eagerly as they rattled off stories from my past. Jami smiled and laughed easily around them. Even when she confessed sheepishly that she was not a great cook, she readily grinned and added, "But I'm one of the best dishwashers you'll ever meet!" They cracked up and gave her credit for her candor and her humor. *Well, we can always order out,* I thought. Jami fit right in with my family, and she appreciated how Gary shaped me.

Again, my mom gave her approval, and though I hadn't been worried about Jami winning her over, it was comforting that my mom also saw how Jami could be my future wife.

Within a year, I knew teaching and coaching would be a part of my lifetime journey. I wanted to make a greater immediate impact, and when I shared my next big dream with Jami, she was all in. She started doing what she did best: thinking of all the details to turn dreams to reality.

* * *

After one year of teaching and coaching cross country at Carroll, which was a private Catholic school, I decided to teach at a nearby public elementary school. I was excited to teach students who had similar backgrounds as mine. I also wanted to expand my reach as a coach, and I had a brewing idea to make that happen.

But now I wanted to expand my reach and coach cross country in the fall. I loved cross country as a runner, and I aimed to influence young runners to fall in love with it, too. My idea was to take a core group of dedicated distance runners at St. Gabriel's and create a Junior Olympic running team, running cross country in the fall and track in the spring. At St. Gabriel's, our mascot was the Redwings, so naturally I wanted to keep that identity.

"So, what's our timeline?" Jami asked.

"Well, I think if I can raise $16,000 in the next two months, we'll be able to take the team to the regional championships at the end of October. And by then, we'll have a good idea about how many kids are at the level where they could compete at nationals, and we can estimate how much we need to allocate to those expenses." I had already looked up the registration fees for both the regional and national meets, calculating the budget in my head.

"And where will the team train? Some places will probably require permits and payments. Where will we get the money from? And what about insurance in case one of the kids gets hurt?" Jami continued her barrage of questions. I smiled. She loved thinking through every detail, while I loved relishing the big picture and the pie-in-the-sky dream. We were like yin and yang when we were focused on a project together. Our strengths were different, yet we were energized by what the other brought to the table. And we respected each other for that.

"I haven't gotten to all that yet, but I was thinking we could call the team the 'DC Redwings' and it can be a year-round team. But any kid can join, not just kids who go to St. Gabriel's. DC doesn't have any youth teams for distance running. There's only one youth track team here, and they have no interest in joining forces with us," I said to Jami as I continued to forge my dream and vision.

Two days earlier, I had stopped by the local high school track where the sole youth track team in DC held their practices. The head coach was an older, pepper-gray-haired gentleman who had been coaching for decades. I introduced myself and proposed my idea to merge some of my runners with his team.

"Hey, Coach, I would love to find a way for us to work together. I coach the St. Gabriel's Redwings, and we have some really dedicated runners who would love to run track after their school season is over. I'm looking to coach year-round as well, especially coaching distance runners."

He looked at me briefly, then said scruffily, "No thanks, son. Why would I want to merge with you? I like running my team the way I've been running it. Good luck though." He turned and walked back toward the infield.

I walked away, feeling dejected and disrespected. I had been under the guise of older, wiser coaches such as Chief and Moultrie, and I thought I still needed that. Surprisingly, once I got past my hurt feelings, the rejection sparked my competitive spirit. *I guess I'm on my own for this. I'll show him.*

I didn't know how I was going to raise the money to buy uniforms and pay our local, regional, and national meet registration fees, but I knew I would find a way. I was making pennies as a teacher, so I also wouldn't be able to pay for everything myself. However, most of my Howard University classmates graduated, were making competitive salaries, and were well connected. I sat down at my kitchen table and wrote down the name and phone number of every person I knew from college. My first strategy would be to ask them and everyone they knew to donate.

It was fall of 1998, and the DC Redwings Youth Program had planted its roots. "It starts with track and ends with success," Jami's best friend Allyceia said when we were brainstorming ideas in those early days. She coined our motto, which quickly became our mantra.

I trained the inaugural DC Redwings team four days a week, two hours each practice. Most of our practices were at one of several local parks, and I made sure I was the first one at every practice to greet each kid as they arrived. It gave me time to chat with them, to see how their day was going, and to joke around.

Kids like Dominique Lockhart and Michael Johnson gave me energy. Dominique was a quiet but very observant eight-year-old. She was lean, and her stride was powerful. Michael was short for his age, but his stride was long. Even at nine years old, his swag made him magnetic. They were kind and loving kids, and they didn't even know how good they could really be. They trusted me and always gave their best. They never questioned a workout, and when I saw doubt creeping into their eyes, I would give them a good story from my days in Gary, which the kids began to call "Garytales."

"When there's no more water in the house, you gotta go out and get it! You gotta go to the well! Come on guys, you can do it. Let's go to the well!" My runners must have thought I was just a big kid. They chuckled at my stories, getting a kick out of my metaphors and my Gary and Howard running days. My "going to the well" exhortation was a go-to. I often followed it with a recollection of one of my hardest workouts when I was a runner. These stories helped me connect to the kids because I was sharing parts of my life that resembled theirs. I didn't mind revealing my vulnerability—my journey, my mistakes and my tough days as a runner, as a student, as a person trying to navigate life.

"Come on, James!"

"You can do this, Donald!"

"Ashley, I want you leading this one!"

My encouragement was constant. The runners, ages ranging from six to fourteen, would respond in the work-out, pushing themselves physically and mentally. By doing so at such young ages, they were heading toward a promising horizon.

I looked forward to every moment I coached. Rain, sleet, or snow—nothing prevented me from getting to practice. I was accustomed to practicing even on the tough days; I applied the same mindset to coaching.

By December, our little team had twelve national qualifiers. Not only had we raised enough money to pay for all of the meet fees, but we also raised enough money for the team to have uniforms, red and black warmup suits, winter running hats and gloves, quality training shoes, racing cleats, and travel duffle bags. We looked like a real team! We were headed to Knoxville, Tennessee, for the 1998 National Junior Olympic Cross Country Championships. I had my pep talk ready, but I was nervous.

I started out by huddling the team and peering down into the group. "Hey, guys, let's go out here and have some fun. Just do your best! Run in your packs as much as you possibly can. Stay relaxed, okay? Get into a good rhythm and fight to the end! Now, come on! Who are we?"

"Redwings!" they all responded in unison.

"Now let's go!" I yelled.

The bantam girls, ages ten and under, lined up first. Dominique Lockhart and Ashley Seymour were my two strongest runners in this division. They were incredibly coachable, possessing an aptitude to follow coaching instructions and to use their instincts to know when to push themselves mentally and physically. They were each pretty quiet but easily laughed at my jokes and aimed to be the best.

As they lined up for their 3K race, my stomach was in knots. *This is crazy,* I thought. *You would think I was the one lining up to run.* I was more nervous waiting for their race to start than I had ever been as a runner. This was the biggest stage I had ever coached on.

What happened next was a blur. Two hundred-plus runners toed the line. The gun went off, and Ashley, Dominique, Lindsay Benjamin, and the other young runners raced ahead, eventually forming small packs that collectively looked like a stream winding through the park, around bends and up hills. Age group after age group raced this way, and after a few hours, my little team was waiting for the awards to be announced. Despite our best efforts, we didn't walk away with any team trophies or awards, and I could tell my little girls and guys were crushed. They all had a befuddled look—like, *Did that just happen*? I don't blame them; I had the same look.

We had some strong finishes during the qualifying meets in the previous weeks but quickly learned that day in Knoxville that running against teams from California, New York, and Illinois, to name a few, was an entirely different game.

Ashley, Dominique, and Lindsay all had respectable finishes for their first time on such a big stage. Michael Johnson, my top runner in the boys ten-and-under division, finished ninth out of more than three hundred runners. I knew he was talented, and he had worked really hard, but we were both shocked at how well he did. He had never run on a national level, yet he responded positively to the competition.

I huddled back up with the team before we boarded the bus to make the long drive back to DC.

"Hey, guys, listen, no heads down, you hear me? I'm really proud you made it to this meet. For most of you, this is your first time ever running cross country. You're still learning. You're stronger and faster, and you've worked harder than you ever have before. And most importantly, you had fun and challenged yourselves. We are proud of ourselves because of the work we put in or, like now, the work we plan to put in! And remember, we're Redwings! We always figure out how we can get better!"

And that's what we did over the next three years. I invited kids of all abilities to join the team. I created a coaching staff and trained them. I became obsessed with building a running program that could take kids with little to no running experience and build them up to compete at high levels. I was all in. And eventually, we got bigger, and we got better.

* * *

"Oh, my goodness, I can't get ready for practice if my phone keeps ringing," I said to Jami with exasperation. She patiently listened to me rant. "They should know I don't cancel," I continued as I shook my head. Rain or shine, our team time trials were still on. But we didn't get either. We got six inches of snow. My response to each parent that called was the same.

"Yes, I see the snow. . . . Everyone should dress in layers so they can peel off their clothing as they warm up. . . . Don't forget a hat and gloves and their team color shirt. . . . Mmm-hmm, mmm-hmmm. . . . They'll be fine. . . . See you soon!"

By the time I got to the park, I felt like a kid in a candy store. *This is Indiana weather.* The snow-covered trees and the glistening field flooded me with memories. This was our critically important intrasquad meet, and weeks prior to this day my assistant coach Tim McMahon and I meticulously strategized the set-up of each of the coed teams. This time trial would give us a barometer for where our kids were for the next major meet. It would simulate a competition atmosphere and would help us determine how to modify the training plan to ensure optimal performance at the right time.

"Let's have them race two loops around Fort Circle Park, then have them come back with a one-loop race," Tim suggested. Fort Circle was a small park with a 1,200-meter loop that sat in the Northwest quadrant of DC. The 2,400-meter and 1,200-meter races were perfect preparation for 2002 nationals, which would take place in Carrollton, Georgia.

"Yep, love that idea," I replied. "We can do three teams and have them wear the same color shirts representing their team. They can even come up with their own team names."

We looked like two little kids putting our Christmas lists together for Santa. We planned with excitement as we maneuvered the names and played out the race to ensure the teams were evenly matched, which would enhance the competition.

Tim started out as an involved and helpful parent at St. Gabriel's but evolved into one of my volunteer assistant coaches. He was average height, and although he no longer had the slender build of his formative years, he had run cross country growing up, and now his son, Quentin, was one of the DC Redwings. Tim was typically easygoing, but he lit up when we debated cross country strategies, and he loved being on the course as much as I did. Because of his quick wit and deep knowledge of the sport, I really appreciated coaching with him.

As we finalized the list of teams, we gave each other a high-five. Then, Tim gestured toward the box I had set down on the cleared patch of grass. "So, the awards came in on time, huh?"

"Barely. Came in day before yesterday. First place team gets trophies, and the other teams get silver and bronze medals."

We had it all planned out—except the four inches of snow we received the night before the intrasquad meet and the two additional inches we received a couple of hours before our practice.

But I didn't skip a beat. I was used to this weather. I trained in it and all types of inclement conditions. I would always tell my runners, "This is Indiana weather!" and "This is championship weather!" I wanted to infuse them with what I learned in Gary. I wanted them to be mentally tough and not to allow any obstacles to get in their way. It was my opportunity to teach them life lessons—the same ones I learned through running, the ones that built my internal and mental toughness.

Four years had passed since I coached our first little DC Redwings team at the national meet in Knoxville, and since then, I had dedicated myself to learning the craft of coaching. I had devoured coaching books, gone to as many coaching clinics and conferences as I could afford, and pestered more experienced coaches with questions to get their advice and learn from them. I had built a year-round youth running team of nearly one hundred runners that provided a culture of excellence and a genuine family atmosphere. I loved my runners. I knew that for so many of them, I had become a father figure and a mentor. My hope was they would look up to me in the same way I looked up to Chief.

The rest of our coaching staff arrived just before the team and trudged through the snow to set up. We set up the awards on a table, marked the course to ensure no corners could be cut, and staked the finishing chute into the ground.

"Oh, my goodness. This is so crazy, Des!" Jami said, shaking her head, half worried and half amused. I grinned.

She knew how deeply committed I was and that no one would talk me out of anything I set my mind to. She had been there with me since the beginning, helping to fundraise, organizing board meetings once we grew into a nonprofit, and coaching and mentoring runners. Many nights, Jami would wake up and find me still working, looking up meet results, designing workouts, or reading up on the latest training methods. When she would accuse me of being somewhat obsessive, I replied I simply wanted to be the best because the kids deserved it and because someone sacrificed for me to have a chance at a better life.

As the runners arrived, some eagerly jumped out of their cars, excited for this unusual chance to test their strength in the snow. A few looked hesitant, expecting I would come to my senses and cancel the time trial.

I gathered them and began my pep talk, beaming as I exhaled into the cold air. "We are going to have some fun today. This is Indiana weather! This is the weather where champions are born. This is a test to see if we really want to perform our best at nationals in a couple weeks. We need this tune-up, and we need you to give your best. Because you even showed up, that tells me you've got some Gary blood in your DNA!" A few chuckled, and a few rolled their eyes.

"Oh, no, not another Gary story!" said Donald Lockhart, Dominique's older brother.

Before I could start again and mesmerize them with a Garytale, a few of our younger runners started to look away, pointing in another direction. With their eyes lit up, more runners started to chatter.

"Whoa! Look at that! Dang!"

"I want one! Wow!"

By now, only half the team was paying attention to me. They were distracted by the display of trophies and medals on the table. A couple of kids gave their teammates a nudge with an elbow or a nod signifying, *Let's go. Time to grind today*!

"Can we race in our sweatpants?" asked Kyle Graves, one of the leading runners in our ten-and-under age group.

I replied, "Sure. But if you race in them, they will get wet and heavy and slow you down. So, I wouldn't recommend it."

"Oh, naw, I'll take them off before the race," he said. "We're going to win today!" he exclaimed with a shy grin.

I don't remember which team won. Was it the Red team? Black? White? I do remember that Coach McMahon and I analyzed our runners so closely and aligned the three inter-squad teams so perfectly that it came down to the wire. It was just a practice we organized like a meet, but the intensity matched any national level meet we had ever been to. Runners walked away with either a first, second, or third place award. And they walked away feeling proud that they had elevated their mental and physical toughness by defeating Mother Nature and her six inches of cold, wet, white snow.

Two weeks later, Kyle and his ten-and-under age-group teammates went on to win the 2002 USA Track & Field Junior Olympic National Championships in Georgia. We also won the eleven- and twelve-year-old boys division and had several top finishers in other age groups who claimed All-American awards.

Just a few months before that monumental time trial in the snow, Jami and I were married on Howard's campus. It was a sunny, hot, and beautiful day when we exchanged our vows. Jami finished her undergraduate studies in 2000 and had become a fifth-grade teacher. She was coaching alongside me and was organizing our growing team and nonprofit. I was teaching at Eugene Clark, a local elementary school, and coaching several sports there. My Clark team dominated the DC Public Schools league, and many of them joined the Redwings since our team trained and competed all year. Coaching had become my life 24/7. And the DC Redwings had become our family. At our wedding on August 3, 2002, a third of the 320 guests attending were DC Redwings runners and their families. And as the reception ended, the skies opened, and the most beautiful summer rain sealed our day.

The day after our wedding, instead of boarding a plane for our honeymoon, we got on a charter bus with almost fifty of our most competitive runners and headed back to

Knoxville, this time for the Amateur Athletic Union Track and Field National Championships. And this time, we were better prepared than our first trip as a team to the Volunteer State. We captured a sizable number of individual and team medals, including a few national titles. Jami and I like to joke that we had two honeymoons—one with fifty kids for seven days at the track and a second a week later where we finally relaxed in sunny Barbados as newlyweds.

With the help of other coaches, such as Lonice Ross, who was my teammate at Howard, and Sherman Turner, an enthusiastic parent I recruited, we would go on to become one of the most dominant youth track and field and cross country programs in the nation. We would claim the AAU Club and Team National Championships in Orlando, Florida, in 2004 and many more national accolades.

But it wasn't about the wins or the losses. It was more about the life lessons that came before, during, and after the competitions. I learned how to create a strong team culture in which kids felt they belonged and ran for one another, just like my experience with my teammates at Horace Mann. I learned how to balance challenging runners to work hard with creating a fun atmosphere. I didn't spend time talking about winning; it was a byproduct of the culture we created. There were friendships and bonds created that extended beyond the track.

I still have DC Redwings runners who keep in touch with me, and a few have even become coaches themselves. I am beyond proud that we built up to more than a hundred runners a year from all over the DC, Maryland, and Virginia area and am humbled by the lives we changed with the sport of running.

CHAPTER 17

WHAT'S THE COST?

———

Bam, bam, bam!

I sprung up in a daze, unclear whether I had heard something at the front door or whether I was dreaming. I peeked at the clock, my head still in a fog. After a double look, I wiped my eyes and confirmed it was early. It was 6:32 on Sunday morning. We had just returned with the team from Orlando after competing at the 2004 AAU Nationals Track and Field Championships, and we were exhausted from the trip.

Bam, bam, bam! "Dez, get out here!" my neighbor Allen yelled. "They're taking your car!"

I threw on a pair of shorts and the nearest T-shirt I could grab, but by the time I raced outside, Allen was standing in a defiant protest with a driver who had our light gray Toyota Corolla strapped to the back of a tow truck. Allen waved his hands in front of him and pleaded with the driver.

"Come on, man! These are hardworking young folks! Give them a break!"

The husky man responded, "Sorry, man. If I give them a break, I lose my job. Does that make sense? Now get out of the way!"

I chimed in, "Come on, sir. You don't have to do this. Not today, not right now!" In the midst of my plea, he cautiously drove away, attempting not to hit Allen. Tears stung my eyes, and when I turned around, I could see tears trickling down Jami's cheeks. She made it outside just in time to see our car being towed away. I turned and mumbled a weak word of thanks to Allen for his attempt to help.

Jami and I trudged back into the house with our heads down, faces sullen, looking at the card the driver had given us. Before I could dial the number, Jami hit me with a barrage of questions.

"What just happened here? Why did he take the car? How can he do that?" She looked at me pleadingly.

I sat down on the couch and took a deep breath and a huge gulp, attempting to clear the lump in my throat. I stumbled with my words but managed to begin to explain, "Remember how I told you that a few of the runners couldn't afford to pay for the Orlando trip? Well, we couldn't leave any kids behind. Besides, if they didn't go, then the relay teams would not have been able to compete, and then what about the other kids?" I paused and rubbed my eyes, still hoping this had not just happened.

"I thought I had more time, but . . . and then Anthony's grandmother told me he needed another pair of racing spikes. So, we—you and I—kinda sponsored four kids, and it prevented us from paying the car note the last three months. I'm really sorry, baby."

Jami sighed slowly and deeply. She knew we were on the same page. We vowed years ago that we would never let money prevent a kid from joining the team or from traveling to the meets, even if it meant that the funds had to come out of our own pockets. We had our water cut off before—and the gas, too. But never for too long. She never complained too much about it, but this time, her worry and concern were different. I was in over my head and in too deep with coaching.

She paced back and forth in front of me, wearing down the living room carpet, deep in thought while she massaged her temples. After about a minute, she gently sat down on the other end of the couch. She took another deep breath and caught my gaze. "What are we going to do? We can't keep doing this. We have more than ourselves to worry about now." Her voice drifted off as she put her face in her hands.

"I know, I know," I said. Jami was four months pregnant. We were elated, but I knew she still worried. She had a miscarriage the previous year, three months into the pregnancy, and she still didn't feel like she could enjoy this upcoming stage in our lives yet. She told me she worried about having another miscarriage while she also dealt with uncertainty about being able to manage her last year of grad school and teaching at the same time. She was already burdened by stress, and this car dilemma didn't help matters.

"Look, I know you love coaching, but we can't live this way. You spend so much time on coaching, you just have nothing left for me—for us." I hated seeing Jami like this, but I didn't have a response that would ease her worries.

By this time, I was still coaching and running the DC Redwings program year-round. I was also teaching PE at a nearby middle school and working as the school's athletic director. At the same time, I had taken a high school coaching job in Greenbelt, Maryland, at Eleanor Roosevelt High School that created a seventy-minute, round-trip commute five to six days a week.

"Dez, you're doin' too much," my mom would say. "You barely have time to call and check on me every once in a while, you're so busy."

"It's too much, baby. We never have any down time. It's just 24/7," Jami would declare.

Most of the time, I would resent those comments. In fact, sometimes I got angry. *I'm trying to make a difference. Can't they see that? My mom just doesn't understand, and Jami just likes to nag. She knows how important coaching is to me.* Other times, I would recommit myself to planning fun dates with Jami or getting home early from practice to surprise her. I tried to make sure to call my mom more often to chat about what was going on in Gary and to check up on my family there.

And then my life changed on that cold Wednesday morning. It was January 26, 2005.

"Baby, I think it's time," Jami spoke into the fleeting peace of the early morning as she slowly swung her feet over the side of the bed before she lifted herself upright. I sprung up, and it was go time.

Nine hours later, our beautiful baby boy was born. Niles Desmond Dunham. Witnessing his birth was like watching God create a miracle right in front of my eyes. His first cry brought tears to my eyes. He was seven and a half pounds and seventeen inches long. His head was full of dark black hair, and every finger and toe was accounted for. My mom was in the delivery room with us. She had been waiting for a grandchild for a long time; she couldn't be happier and cried her own set of tears.

Every night Jami was in the hospital with Niles, I slept in the tiny hospital bed with her, not wanting to leave her side or our precious little baby. I still went to track practice though, only missing it on the day Niles was born. I was beaming, telling everyone about my new son. I wanted to share this good news with anyone who would listen! All my runners volunteered to babysit and were excited to meet baby Niles.

The next six months whizzed by. Jami and I got into a routine with our new son and new life as parents. Our mothers were extremely helpful, both of them tag-teaming to stay with us during this transition. I now had even more to look forward to at track meets. Whenever she could, Jami would come to the meets with baby Niles in tow. He quickly became a team mascot of sorts. The runners and families loved holding him and playing with him. I would look up in the stands and feel so proud of my little family. I felt a renewed sense of purpose. I wanted to be better for them. I wanted to work harder to provide for them. It was a love I never knew I would experience.

* * *

"Daddy's gone, Dez," my sister Shnicks cried. "He didn't make it through the night," she continued to sob.

I clinched the phone tightly in my hand and sat down on my couch. My heart began to race, and my breathing shifted. When we got off the phone, I immediately dialed Jami. It was August, and she was at her school while I was home alone with Niles. I barely choked out the news to Jami and then hung up when she said she was on her way. With tears streaming down my face, I went into Niles' nursery and picked him up from his crib.

My dad had been struggling with lung cancer and a plethora of other drinking related issues for a few years. By the time Niles was born in January, my dad's health had declined drastically. My dad met Niles when he was about seven months old, just a few weeks before my dad lost his battle to cancer. I never got closure before my dad died. There was so much I needed to say.

I learned a few years earlier that I had a younger brother named Preston. My dad kept this information from me, and even after I learned the truth, Preston was never mentioned. My dad cheated me out of many experiences, including being a big brother. By the time I met Preston, he was in high school, and I was teaching and living in DC. I immediately saw in him our dad's tall and slender build, his eyes, his cheekbones. When he spoke, he did so with our dad's cadence. Sadness, loss, anger, and hope flooded me simultaneously.

I know my dad loved me. I know he struggled with some serious demons. I never got to tell him how his struggles created trauma in my life and in my siblings' lives and how much I resented that. I have worked on that resentment, but for a long time, I struggled to trust anyone. I struggled through relationships for years and clawed my way to a healthy, sustainable marriage.

It was a juxtaposition; the same year I became a dad, I lost mine. That August day, I lay holding my baby boy on my chest, clutching him with emotion that had more to do with what I lost in my childhood than what I lost that day. That was the moment I vowed to be the best father possible to Niles.

CHAPTER 18

CHAMPIONSHIP WEATHER

———

What else? What am I missing? Should I change this workout?

As I sat on my couch, papers surrounding me with times and training logs, I incessantly looked at my workout plan for each phase of the season. I had to get it right. Again, I was up at nearly two o'clock in the morning. It was early September, just a couple weeks after my dad died. I was studying and strategizing in preparation for the next cross country meet that my team from Eleanor Roosevelt would run in.

I shook my head just thinking about it. We couldn't have a repeat of the 2004 cross country season finale. After finishing third in our region in 2004, I was confident that we would be one of two teams in the final countdown for selection to compete at the Nike Team Nationals cross country meet, but the committee had another idea. The twenty-team national field was selected by a designated committee formed by Nike. The top two teams from the eight regions automatically qualified, and then an additional four at-large teams were chosen. Only one Maryland team was invited to the party—and it wasn't us.

C. Milton Wright High School was bestowed the honor, although we outran them by an average of twenty-three seconds per runner at the Maryland state meet. We were in separate divisions, so we did not get the opportunity to compete head-to-head. C. Milton Wright had performed well throughout the season and had a strong schedule, and we ran the same course about an hour apart. Even though both teams toed the starting line on the same day and ran the same course at the same meet and we ran faster, those facts didn't sway the selection committee.

We couldn't help but feel disheartened. Our girls had trained forty to fifty miles per week for most of the summer and fall. They trained hard, but it wasn't enough. We weren't selected. And boy did that hurt.

C. Milton Wright went on to race against the best of the best in Portland, Oregon, where runners received VIP treatment as they graced the Nike Headquarters Campus and hung out in the amazing Tiger Woods Center. Flight, hotels, plush apparel, and meals were all taken care of by Nike. It stung to end our season prematurely. I questioned my schedule and meet selections and felt I didn't put the team in the best position to get the early quality votes. *What could I have done differently?*

"Baby, are you coming to bed soon?" Jami asked from upstairs, breaking my train of thought.

"Yeah, baby, in a bit." But my mind was racing, and it would take time for it to settle enough to fall asleep. Besides, I knew Niles would wake up soon, and I enjoyed those middle-of-the-night moments with him, changing his diaper, cuddling and kissing him, and then taking him to his mom for her to nurse him before he went back to sleep.

Jami was used to this, but she still grew concerned when I became consumed with one of my teams. A few months earlier, during one of many conversations about my time being dominated by coaching, Jami tried to persuade me to see things from her perspective.

"Baby, something's gotta give. You're coaching three teams, and your family needs you. I need you home more," Jami pleaded late that summer after Niles was born. I did not want to end our run with the DC Redwings, but deep down I knew I couldn't be stretched as thin anymore. I knew my marriage couldn't handle it, either. *I know. She's right. Something has to give.*

So, at the end of 2005, accompanied by much anguish and heartbreak, we ended an eight-year era of youth running in DC. We made the decision to shutter the DC Redwings. My focus now fully shifted to building the program at Eleanor Roosevelt. I was completely focused on training the distance runners at Eleanor Roosevelt, and as an assistant coach in the program, I was able to specialize in event areas near and dear to my heart.

* * *

The 2005 Hartford Invitational beckoned in just a week, and we had to be ready. As I continued to survey my training notes on the couch, I did a mental checklist, hoping my previous two seasons of learning at Roosevelt reflected in my plan.

Early season quality meets. *Check.* Mentally tougher. *Check.* Top returning runners are back and stronger than ever. *Check.*

Our team was up bright and early that next Saturday, loaded in vans headed to the Hartford Invitational in Bel Air, Maryland. We were gunning for two powerhouse teams— Delaney High School and our nemesis, C. Milton Wright.

The hour-long ride was quiet. With no traffic, I sped down the highway, the fall foliage in my peripheral view, my mind previewing the race, anticipating which places I thought each of our girls could finish, and calculating what our score needed to be in comparison with our competitors. Our girls knew this meet could stamp their ticket to Nike Team Nationals. The Hartford Invitational was the meet that could reconcile the snub from the previous year.

As we pulled into the parking lot, I could see the multi-colored flags lining the finishing chute. *Here we go. This is it. They're ready.* The tension was thick. No joking, no laughing. The girls filed out of the vans with stoic faces, ready to prove themselves. The slight chip on their shoulders armed them with an attitude reflecting the determination with which they would step onto the course.

Once our girls started warming up, I became antsy and felt the steady climb of my anxiety. I marked the spots on the course where I would coach during the race, giving my cues and encouragement to the girls as they ran. *Come on girls. You can do this.*

The varsity girls race started, and I was already sweating despite the cool, brisk weather. And because I could never stand still and coach my team, I probably ran as many miles as my athletes did, zigzagging where I could on the spectator portions of the course, trying to catch key moments when I could yell encouragement and strategy to my runners.

With conviction, Dominique Lockhart and Marika Walker from our team landed a fierce one-two punch in 17:21 and 17:23 for three miles, followed by Teshika Rivers, who finished as our third runner. Dominique had been with me since her youth running days at St. Gabriel's, so I knew she had nerves of steel. Marika was an unassuming runner with a quiet demeanor. She stumbled across running when her soccer dreams were cut short by a broken ankle in the fall of her freshman year. She began her running career as a 6:40 miler and didn't look back. The rest of the varsity squad included Tyreka Arrington, Nayda Pirela, Tunisia Milner, Jennifer Redman, Tasha Stanley, and Christine Danielson.

Our team stood out. Our top runners were Black, and they had me, a Black head coach. It wasn't something you saw often on the cross country courses in Maryland or on the national level during the early 2000s.

In running events, culturally and historically, Black runners have not been encouraged to run cross country. Basketball, football, and the short sprints in track and field have provided the most role models for Black kids in sports. Recreational running is touted as a way of life for White, middle-class, and wealthy families. Where I grew up, if you saw someone running in the neighborhood, it wasn't for recreation, and you certainly took the cue and ran too—ask questions later! As a runner and then as a coach, I took pride in dispelling the stereotypes and disrupting the myths that Black kids can't run long distances.

The 2005 performance at the Hartford Invitational sky-rocketed our crew into the conversation of national rankings. But there is always more building and growing to do. The workouts were proving spot on, so my focus narrowed in on our culture. We would be as fit as any team at nationals, but would we be mentally strong? I would soon find my answer.

One day, a few weeks after that Hartford win, we went on a moderately paced eight-mile run during practice, with the coaches joining the girls on this cold and rainy day. It had rained all day, and the fields held on to the rain, causing some deep puddles. Initially the girls attempted to navigate the puddles, but they were quickly reminded that second-place teams worry about obstacles and champions run through them.

"Come on y'all, let's go!" I encouraged them. Other coaches joined in.

"This is what champions are made of," Coach Sherman chimed in. "Let's go!"

I made a last-minute decision to alter the workout, abandoning our plan to run a scenic route beyond the school and instead continuing our run around the same field over and over again. This was strategic. A talkative group became silent, and I had their full attention. Their focus and concentration became more intense as they looped around the muddy field with nearly calf-deep puddles.

"If you can run in these conditions, you can run in any conditions!" I said between breaths. I knew they were cold and couldn't feel their feet at this point. The twenty-plus laps around the small field in bone-chilling, freezing rain and blustery winds would be a practice they would never forget. It was a long and painful run as they tried to coordinate each step with the unpredictable footing. This was the moment when we saw their physical ability align with their heart and souls. It wasn't the endless 800-meter, 1,200-meter, or 1,600-meter repeats; it was the cold, rain, and mud that transformed them.

They became gladiators that day, and we all knew it. We could see, and we could *feel* the transcendence into an invincible force. All you heard was heavy breathing, feet sloshing through the mud and pounding through the puddles. Play time was over. Talking ceased until there was encouragement about not allowing any space between the tight pack of eight.

"Space means visitors, and there are no visitors allowed," Teshika retorted. "Now close it up!" And the girls followed her command. She was referencing a race strategy we had taught them, and I was proud to see her leadership in this moment. These girls were on a mission, and they were all prepared for battle, in rhythm with each other.

"This is championship weather! Days like this, champions stay focused on their goals," I urged. This type of training and philosophy had to become the backbone of our program if we wanted to be national-level contenders. But the principles also had the potential to extend beyond the sport as they navigated their futures.

The co-existence of challenge and reward, I realized, was the simple reason I fell in love with running. No other sport ever gave me that feeling. In spite of teammates and competitors, the sport of running is truly you against yourself. When you conquer your internal stoicism, you're left with this almost cynical self-satisfaction of knowing you just conquered yourself. This elusive reward dangles like a carrot in front of you to chase, to reach the dream of wanting more of that scintillating feeling of accomplishment. This is what my assistant coaches and I wanted embedded in our runners—this mindset, this attitude, and this grit every time they raced and, more importantly, for the curveballs that life throws us all.

As the 2005 season went on, we positioned ourselves as top contenders to be selected to Nike Team Nationals. When we ran in a nationally competitive meet at the historic Van Cortlandt Park in the Bronx, New York, we took fifth in a star-studded field. We did our job, and our ranking reflected it. We climbed the charts the entire season and were next in line to get the nod for nationals. We were anxious as we awaited the penultimate rankings but had a feeling of accomplishment. We did all we could do, our best, and next, we would prepare for a state meet that would not carry any weight for the national rankings but could give us back-to-back Maryland state championships.

The following week, we exuded confidence the day before the rankings announcement as we ran and chanted that we were going to the national championship. Over and over throughout the run, we proudly sang, "We goin' to the ship! We goin' to the ship!"

The next day, a Saturday, I eagerly checked the Dyestat website to view the updated rankings. I was stunned. Somehow, a Virginia team had undeservingly jumped us in the rankings.

I immediately called Coach Sherman. "This is bullshit, man!" I spewed when he answered the phone.

I knew the Virginia team did not have the strength of schedule we had, and in a cross-meet analysis, they didn't come close to our accomplishments.

"Their schedule is whack! We would kill them head-to-head. This just makes no sense!" I continued. I again felt like we were getting short-changed. *Are we being underestimated because of what we look like?* I couldn't help but wonder.

Sherman agreed, and we both hung up, dumbfounded. We would not get an opportunity to race against the Virginia team, and we had no other meets left in the season that would feature a team with enough weight to bump us up one more notch. Our upcoming state meet wouldn't have enough national-level teams.

Not being selected in 2004 was extremely disappointing. So, this year we knew we had to work harder. And we planned so diligently that we were 100 percent convinced we would be selected. When we weren't, we were certain we had been screwed out of a trip to Portland. I emailed the committee members at Nike, but the response I received was not favorable. We were unfairly denied.

At the next practice, we broke the news to the girls, who were rightfully devastated.

"This isn't fair!" Tunisia said as the other girls nodded.

"But we did better than some of those other teams," Nayda added.

"I know," was all I could muster. They had done everything they were supposed to do and clearly outperformed teams that went into the postseason in a premium position.

The decision was inexplicable from an athletic perspective, but it became a major life lesson for all of us. After the letdown, we spent the next couple of days attempting to refocus on the Maryland state cross country championship.

"Sometimes you do all you can and it's still not enough," I said during one of our team huddles. "We can only control our efforts. And you should still be proud. You worked extremely hard. Life is not fair, but we still get to decide how we respond to it. So, let's keep our heads up and get ready for what's next." I was still seething about the decision, but I knew I needed to set the tone for how to deal with such a disappointment. We concluded the week of practice with easy running and were careful not to add any additional stress on the girls.

The next Saturday, I received a frantic call from Coach McMahon. "They ran! They ran! Unbelievable, they ran and lost!"

"Huh, what are you saying, Tim?" I could barely understand what he attempted to share.

"The Virginia team ran and lost to an unranked team! They went to New York for a low-key meet and lost!" My mouth dropped, and I jumped up, pumping my fists in the air. The Virginia team could not retain their ranking after suffering a defeat to an unranked team. This would allow us to return to our rightful position.

We couldn't wait to tell the girls, and when we did, they screamed for joy! The chant returned, "We goin' to the ship! We goin' to the ship!" This was the happiest I had ever seen the team.

Fast forward a week to early November. We captured our second straight state championship, and Marika won her first individual state championship on the infamous Hereford course. Hereford High School, located in Parkton, Maryland, was known as one of the toughest courses in the country, and it included a massive hill that runners had to conquer at the beginning and the end of the race. The course was truly designed for the runners with the most grit. It was agony, pure torture, but it also rendered the question, "Who wants it the most?"

With renewed confidence, we flew out to Portland the first weekend in December. The weather conditions were dreadful, to say the least. There had been torrential downpours in the days before our arrival, and they hadn't stopped. The course at Portland Meadows Race Track looked like it had been in a monsoon, and it provided an extra test to see whether each of the teams truly wanted to be there. We placed extra clothes in garbage bags to keep them dry while the team previewed the course with a jog. More than anything, I wanted the girls to know they belonged at this meet—they had done all the work, and they were just as good as their competitors.

My mind was put at ease when Dominique exclaimed within the first few strides of warmup, "This is championship weather!" We all chuckled in complete agreement. *Yep, they absolutely belong here.*

Regardless of the outcome of the race, the mission was accomplished. These girls' attitudes reflected the quote, "Life is ten percent of what happens to you and ninety percent how you respond to it." (Swindoll n.d.) We went on to take eleventh overall at nationals, a solid showing, and proved our point that we belonged there, knocking off nine other top twenty teams. Not bad for a team that received the final selection because of a fluke.

CHAPTER 19

LICKING OUR WOUNDS

We headed into the last weekend of April 2006, the traditional weekend for the Penn Relays Carnival, with excitement and anticipation. This meet was the Super Bowl of track meets on the East Coast, and we knew the Jamaican teams would test our abilities. I questioned whether I had successfully prepared my team for what they were about to face.

We had had a great cross country season in the fall and were still feeling solid about our showing at Nike Team Nationals. But the Jamaicans had been so dominant in previous years that we probably had a better chance of winning big with a lottery scratch-off than to haul the "Big Penny" first-place trophy home. Winning teams at Penn Relays are awarded a three-foot-diameter oversized penny that is sought by thousands and thousands of runners each year. Coaches were known to bring rope to the relays in hopes they would be the ones tying the "Big Penny" to the roof of their car or team van.

As a runner at Howard, I was blown away by the atmosphere and competition at Penn Relays. The meet featured the best high school, college, and professional runners from the East Coast and beyond. And now as a coach, I hoped to establish Roosevelt among the best teams. Our girls ran for one another. They ran with heart, complimented by a deliberate and serious physical training regimen.

On the first day of the meet, as I tried to focus on the races and my team's preparation, I couldn't help but be distracted by the dominating presence of the Jamaican teams. Their pre-race warmup was rhythmic and upbeat. They lined up in the infield, each runner striding out about forty meters, every step deliberate and graceful, yet powerful and intense. Every few minutes, runners cranked out a few synchronized running drills or sprints, firing on all cylinders to get them revved up and ready to go. They looked like gazelles, naturally fast and confidently robust. Watching their warmup was very similar to watching a platoon preparing to go to war. They didn't talk much, remaining mostly aloof despite a smirk every so often, and they moved in sync with an air of entitlement, as if they invented the sport of running.

We faced a strong field of teams, including Holmwood Tech High School from Jamaica, in the 1,600-meter relay trials. Takecia, one half of the track-famous Jameson twins, was our anchor leg (the fourth and last runner on the relay team). She was poised as she faced the homestretch and cruised across the finish line in the best preliminary time by an American team, securing our spot in the much-anticipated finals. The Holmwood team still finished seven seconds before us, so we knew a tall order was ahead for the finals the next day.

We fared well during the other preliminary races and headed back to our hotel that evening, ready to rest up for day two.

The next day, we lined up mid-morning for our first final, called a Championship of America at this meet. This race was the 3,200-meter relay, also known as the 4x800-meter relay. The Jamaican teams stepped on the track with a ton of confidence, having captured nineteen of the past twenty Championships of America, and this day would be no different. Holmwood Tech featured Bobby-Gaye Wilkins, a high school junior at the time, who had represented Jamaica at the 2005 World Youth Championships in Athletics. Though we didn't know it then, she would also represent them on a more grandiose stage at the 2008 Olympic Games in Beijing, winning a silver medal in the 1,600-meter relay. (Olympic Games, 2008) Wilkins' teammates were a strong supporting cast of girls who represented their country on a world-championship level.

Our girls did their best to hang on for dear life and were able to muster enough strength to stay with the top teams for three and a half laps of the eight-lap race. After the Jamaican teams pulled away on the second leg, it was clear the American teams were not ready to dethrone the Jamaicans.

The victory whistles began to blow prematurely for the Jamaicans as they led the last four and a half laps. Holmwood Tech crossed the line in eight minutes and forty-five seconds, and we finished third overall, stopping the clock almost eight seconds after Holmwood. Edwin Allen High School, also a Jamaican powerhouse, nudged us by half a second to earn the runner-up spot. It was a great run for our team, and I was extremely proud. How could I not be? They set a school record and clocked the third-fastest time in US girls' history!

Despite mixed emotions, my quartet knew they ran their best. They competed with heart and tenacity but came to the realization that, although they ran an extremely fast and nationally ranked time, they did not have the firepower to top the Jamaicans. Although we trained incredibly hard, we were out-trained and outmatched.

Holmwood Tech grabbed a first-place finish in the 4x100-meter relay next, leaving them in position to earn a triple crown if they could pull off one more win. We would have another shot to face off with them, perhaps to squash their triple crown hopes, with the 1,600-meter relay finals at the end of the day. The odds were a bit better for us in this race. After all, the Jamaicans had captured a mere fifteen of the past twenty-one titles against the American teams in this race.

Much to my chagrin, Holmwood ran an amazing 3:36.09, the third-fastest time ever run at the Penn Relays by a girls high school team. It crushed its own record by two seconds, one that was set in 2001.

The Holmwood team had firepower that was unmatched, including Sonita Sutherland on the anchor leg, and she was a force to be reckoned with. Sonita had set a personal record of 51.13 in the 400 meters earlier in the year. To put it in its proper perspective, she could beat most high school boys in this event. She grabbed the baton and cruised to a 53.2 split for the win, sending a message to our team that we would not forget. Even though we were the top American team, we were not ready for the big leagues just yet. The sun was out that day, shining on the Jamaican teams brighter than ever.

* * *

"Damn! We ran our asses off, and it still wasn't enough! We broke school records, personal records, and gave it everything we had! They were just too tough, bro!" I stopped and took a deep breath. My pride was still tender, and I couldn't pretend otherwise, especially when I had read a bold and brash headline of an article detailing our shortcomings.

Sherman responded, "I know, man. The Jamaican teams have a real advantage, though. They came into Penns coming off a full season, including their Caribbean championships!"

Our sprints coach, Tia Clemmons, interjected, "They are coming to Penn Relays oiled, primed, and ready to rumble when we're just getting into our outdoor season."

Despite running a time most high school girls' teams could only dream of and placing an impressive third in the 4x800 relay, we returned home to a heart-wrenching reality: "Roosevelt Still Has Catching Up to Do" was *The Washington Post*'s headline about the 2006 Penn Relays Track and Field Carnival.

The sting of the loss from the weekend was still poignant. But in a strange way, it was also motivating and exciting. Our girls proved they could run on the big stage, and we had certainly caught the attention of not only the top American teams but a few Jamaican teams as well. I had a whole year now to plan and strategize for 2007, and I was eager to go back to the drawing board.

"We've got to have a better prep meet to get ready," Coach McMahon said. I nodded in agreement. With little contemplation, I knew who we needed to race and exactly where we needed to go to sharpen up for the 2007 Penns.

Come mid-May, a few weeks after the 2006 Penn Relays, we were in an intense coaches' meeting, bantering about how to crack the code of winning at least one of the "Big Pennies" against our Jamaican counterparts. We were fiercely competitive and strove to leave an indelible mark at Franklin Field. We could still hear the ringing of the Jamaican whistles. We could see flags waving. The pride and the confidence of the fans wearing the black, yellow, and green was palpable. The experience was inspiring, but we needed the tables to turn.

Suddenly, a question derailed my train of thought.

"Hey, who's the most dominant American program over the past decade?"

Coach Tuck quickly responded, "LA Long Beach Poly, of course."

Long Beach Poly had a mascot—Jackrabbits—befitting its national success in the long sprints, and most of all, it had won at Penn Relays before. Coached by the legendary Don Norford, also known as Papa Don, Long Beach Poly captured thirteen girls California state championships over almost two decades, eight more than any other school. Papa Don coached a plethora of future NCAA champions and Olympians. (NHS T&F HOF n.d.) His team featured national youth age group stars Turquoise Thompson and Jasmine Joseph. Thompson would go on to become an NCAA Division I All-American and professional runner.

"Yep, Long Beach Poly. The West Coast is where we need to be! It's warm most of the year, and the Arcadia Invitational is a few weeks before Penns. It's the perfect tune-up meet. Plus, I know Long Beach Poly and Long Beach Wilson both go to that meet," I shared with the other coaches.

The Arcadia Invitational featured other top California teams and first-rate national programs from around the country. Running at a premier meet such as Arcadia would be pivotal.

At one of our practices a few days later, Doris Anyawu, the Jameson twins, and Tasha Stanley were stretching and talking again about their Penn Relays experience.

"I just keep thinking about it. Like, maybe I could have worked harder?"

"If I hadn't missed that week during pre-season training . . ."

"I know I had more in me. . . ."

"What else could I have done?"

All these questions loomed in their heads—and mine, too. I constantly wondered what I could have done differently as their coach. I felt the burden of our loss.

Dez, what's missing? What more can you do?

It was time to go to the lab. I needed to study, to analyze, to diagnose every decision leading up to our last performance at Penns. And I had to pull everyone else in to do the same. We needed to study the Jamaicans' training habits, strategies, and insane commitment to the sport. Our training plan needed to be tweaked. With more than three hundred days of razor-focused preparation ahead, our strong foundation would be built, but it would feel like an eternity before our next shot at the "Big Penny."

CHAPTER 20

BOUNCING BACK

———

"So, you think this one meet can make a difference?" Taylor asked, leaning back in his desk chair.

I responded adamantly, "This one meet is definitely a game changer. We don't get much time to take advantage of the warm weather."

I pitched the wild idea of attending the Arcadia meet to our adviser and vice principal at Roosevelt, Avery Taylor, soon after the coaches' meeting. He was our assigned administrator who ran most team administrative duties, including fundraising, and absolutely loved track.

He gave me a second look, took a deep breath and said, "I'm feeling this idea, Dunham." We looked up the 2007 meet date, and it aligned perfectly with our spring break.

As I continued talking, Taylor continued to click away on his computer. A grin spread across his face. The bigger the smile, the harder and faster he typed. He finally asked, "What if we race at Arcadia, then stay and train the following week, and then compete at the Mount Sac Relays after that?"

My mind spun with possibilities. We knew we needed to cover the cost of flights, food, and lodging for the girls and coaches for a whole week, and even if we traveled at budget rates, it was going to be a sizable expense. And this time, I knew Jami would not agree to us covering the costs. We knew parents would pitch in, but we couldn't ask them to carry the burden of such a cost without help. We needed to get creative and turned our efforts into hosting spaghetti dinners and candy sales. If we really hustled and kept our end goal in sight, we knew we could do it.

This trip would allow us to see the best American teams three weeks before Penn Relays. The warm weather and focused training would increase the intensity of our workouts. Training on the East Coast, we always ran the risk of colder weather playing a factor in quality workouts and of potential injury. The warmer California weather would allow us to train twice a day—one practice in the morning and another practice in the evening—providing the atmosphere to work on strategic scenarios such as positioning relay exchanges and race execution.

It was set. We would fly across the country for a critical tune-up before heading back to the East Coast to face off against the Jamaicans again at the 2007 Penn Relays. Heading into the summer of 2006, I was on a mission.

I continued to increase the complexity of my training methods. I traveled to several coaching clinics and learned from prominent coaches, including Marcus O'Sullivan, Clyde Hart, and Karen Dennis. I dug into Boo Schexnayder's training principles and workouts. I studied a variety of strength training regiments. I analyzed top teams' schedules to gain insight into quality meets for optimal performances at the right time. And most of all, I studied the top Jamaican teams—their strategies, their strengths, and any potential weaknesses, though the latter was hard to find.

If you asked any of the girls, they would probably have said: "We work hard and run for each other. It's about having pride." That summer, the training also intensified. More mileage, more days, more practices, calculated paces. Years earlier, I borrowed a pivotal idea from the New York powerhouse distance team Saratoga Springs High School. Following Saratoga's lead, we launched a summer training program. We were restricted from training as a high school team during the summer, so we created a club team, the "Blazin' Raiders," to allow our girls to continue to train and compete as a group.

Our summer training, under the guise of the club, allowed the girls to log the necessary miles to build a solid foundation for the upcoming cross country season. I told our runners that if we're ever going to have a shot at being dominant at Penn Relays, they had to commit to our summer training program, which meant no hard racing with other club teams. If we wanted to do the unimaginable, we had to start an unimaginable workout regimen that summer that would continue into the following spring, when we would face the Jamaican teams again.

My approach was considered somewhat unorthodox. I had all our runners—including our sprinters—train like cross country runners. In other words, they ran distance and ran it often. We modified workouts for some of our sprinters when we needed to, but they still ran the distance. If done properly in a progressive manner, this approach would generate physical, physiological, and especially mental benefits that pure sprinting workouts would not allow. The mental resilience developed through distance was beyond a running skill. It was a skill needed to overcome odds and challenges in life.

To teach our girls race execution, we lined up ten to twelve of them and had them race-walk about twenty meters. Then I would have them freeze. I would randomly point to one of them, prompting the runner to describe and analyze their position followed by their anticipation of what could happen next and how they were going to avoid potential trouble or even get out of trouble. This helped to teach them how to avoid tripping, getting cut off or slowing down by getting trapped by slower runners. If all else failed and one of the above occurred, they knew how to respond. One thing was certain: They knew that panicking or giving up was not an option.

Strategy was critical. Our girls needed not only to run fast, but they also needed to develop racing strategies to counter the Jamaican tactics. We developed workouts to emphasize the third 200 meters of the 800 so our girls could keep the pressure on the field at the start of the second lap. We practiced shifting the pace right at that moment so our girls could develop the capacity to do so when they were winded from the first half of the race. The baton exchange was another key area.

"The stick never slows down, ladies," we would remind them as we practiced baton exchanges. We routinely ended practice with drills to model the proper technique for those important passes between each leg.

Coming off an intense summer training schedule, we had high aspirations for the fall cross country season, and momentum continued to swing our way. We snagged our third straight cross country Maryland 4A state championship, and senior Marika Walker defended her individual title. We even received another bid to Nike Team Nationals and improved our placement to eighth overall.

We went into the new year and the 2007 track season more physically fit than ever. Besides becoming physiologically and muscularly more developed, the girls were tougher mentally, maintained a more positive attitude during tough times and tough workouts, and were determined not to give up.

Our plan to race top-level competition before Penn Relays was in motion. With Taylor's help, we raised enough money and secured the school's approval to fly across the country with a universal goal in mind. In early April, our team of coaches and twenty-four runners, all with matching black and teal team T-shirts, met at the airport at 5 a.m. and boarded our flight to Burbank, California. The girls were still a bit sleepy because of the early hour, but they were excited and chatting and laughing as we waited for our flight to depart.

We didn't realize what we were in for during this coast-to-coast flight.

Jami and our six-month-old daughter, Nia, joined us for the six-hour-plus flight, and it was a laborious one. Nia had eczema and severe allergies and didn't enjoy the dry air or turbulence. She vehemently expressed this to everyone on the plane. Eventually we calmed her down to a manageable state by working as a team. Each runner and coach took turns holding her and pacing with her up and down the aisle when allowed. She finally fell asleep with about fifteen minutes left in the flight.

The team was exhausted from the early rise and long, onerous flight. We quickly checked into our low budget hotel and headed to a neighboring track to loosen up our legs. Upon arriving at the track, we made it clear this was not a field trip. Fun was built in, but the work came first. We took a few laps, executed drills, and stretched well. The key part of the practice was to calm nerves and to review race strategies. The team knew it was okay to race those who were better than them as long as they engaged in good, wholesome competition and allowed that engagement to make them better.

On the first day of racing at the Arcadia Invitational, the big East Coast vs. West Coast showdown took place in the 4x200-meter relay. Long Beach Wilson High School came in as the meet favorite featuring nationally ranked sprinter, Shelise Williams. I perched at the 300-meter mark, where I could give a final yell of encouragement to our second and fourth legs down the last straightaway.

Pow! The runners sprinted out of the blocks. Doris Anyawu kept us in the race, running neck and neck with the top pack the entire first leg. By the time the second legs brought the baton down the homestretch, Tameka Jameson had us in the race as full contenders for a top finish.

"Move, Meka! Pump your arms! Finish strong!" I yelled as she powered around the turn and down the homestretch in her last hundred meters. She kept us in the hunt, with two other teams all within a few feet from one another. I marveled as the crowd stood on its feet, wondering who this East Coast team was.

She was a ball of nerves, but our third leg, Tasha Stanley, grabbed the baton from Tameka and blazed around the curve, staying stride for stride against the national sprint powerhouse Long Beach Wilson. She then handed our anchor leg, Takecia, the baton in perfect position, dead even with Long Beach Wilson. Shelise Williams, Wilson's anchor leg, shot out like a rocket after receiving the baton for the final 200-meter leg, but Takecia would not let her separate. *Come on, Kecia! You got this!* I thought as I waited for her to get closer to where I could shout some encouragement. I'm sure Shelise could feel Takecia's breath literally down her neck.

"Come on, Kecia! Arms! Arms! Stay relaxed!" I shouted as loud as I could over the roaring crowd. Shelise attempted to make a move with one hundred meters to go, seemingly amid panic, but could not shake the Jameson twin as the race came down to a grueling last twenty meters.

Surprisingly, we won over some of the crowd as they cheered for us, the underdog team from the East Coast. Shelise's muscles tightened just steps from the finish line. That was all the oomph Takecia needed to claim a victory by 0.05 seconds. The entire crowd stood on its feet, wildly cheering. *We just upset one of the top US teams in the country. This is unbelievable! Is this plan really going to work?*

The second day of the meet, our major face-off was with Long Beach Poly in the 4x400-meter relay, and the moment of truth, did not disappoint anyone who witnessed it. At this point, we had gained some respect. California spectators began to wish us good luck, hoping we would take down Poly. There weren't many, but enough for us to feel as if we had fans in the stands besides our coaches and parents.

Doris, who was known for her nerves of steel, led us off again, with Stanley and the twins once again rounding out the relay. Takecia pulled away just enough down the straightaway with the crowd roaring and cameras flashing, and a new school record was set. They managed a bit more space to win this relay by 0.5 seconds.

But we weren't done yet. Our week-long trip continued with twice-a-day practices, a delicious dinner at the famous Roscoe's House of Chicken and Waffles, and an overall team win at the Mount Sac Invitational during the culminating weekend.

The week proved we could contend with the top nationally ranked teams. *But were we ready for the Jamaicans?*

CHAPTER 21

HOUSE OF CHAMPIONS

———

Our performance in California confirmed that the months leading up to that point were worth all the time and energy. The girls meant business, turned up their training intensity another notch, and redoubled their commitment.

Our vision for redemption was simple: work hard, strengthen our team and family atmosphere, and establish a true "House of Champions" culture. We introduced the House of Champions concept in the fall after that third-place finish at Penn Relays in 2006. I gave each runner a blue baton to further cement this idea of a true championship culture. The sky blue represented our school colors.

"Your baton must be treated with honor and prestige," I began. "It should never touch the ground, nor should it leave your side. Keep your baton in your possession at all times at practice, during school. At no time should you be without it, or the team will pay the price." They understood that meant agonizing push-ups at the end of each practice. The baton idea was established to remind them of their commitment to one another and to our mission, "Operation Penn Relays 2007," on a daily basis. Our operation challenged them to be the best that they could be in all that they did, especially when they didn't feel up to it. They understood that as a team, their daily actions in school, at practice and meets, at home, and in their community affected one another. It made them understand that life is bigger than themselves and that having humility and thinking of others are the true concepts of team, community, and the human spirit.

We incentivized our runners to go beyond the call of duty in training and in their commitment to one another. That recognition came with our House of Champions honor, which we coined "HOC." To earn this honor, our runners needed to go beyond the call of duty and earn ten stars throughout the course of the season. You could earn stars only by exceeding team tasks and being challenged to a level of discomfort yet still pushing beyond expectations. Tameka was our team captain, and she took this commitment so seriously that she showed up for practice after having two wisdom teeth removed that day. We could barely understand what she was telling us, but once we figured it out, we sent her home immediately to rest for a few days. Those would be the only practices she missed. And, of course, we had to give her stars for that kind of dedication to her team.

Developing the HOC culture was our way to get the runners to buy-in and go beyond their limits as well as our expectations. Upon receiving ten stars, they were awarded the special black T-shirt with light blue HOC letters across the back, one they were proud to wear.

Over the next few months, my fellow coaches and I were able to teach the girls that winning races and championship titles is a byproduct of the lifestyle they and their teammates choose to live. This same spirit was embodied by the Jamaicans; they were representing a bigger picture: their country. And this was what we were up against: teams with an entire country on their shoulders. The Jamaicans walked like it, moved like it, warmed up like it, and if you saw them in the bullpen, they were like the bulls waiting for the gates to go up in a major rodeo. Their focus was sharp, and they always looked the part, as if they belonged in a battle royale.

On the other hand, our team also respected balance. And we sure did need to leverage the concept of balance when we returned to the Penn Relays in April 2007. On day one, torrential rain delayed the start of our big race, so we played card games and entertained ourselves during the idle time while our runners nibbled on Jamaican coco bread to keep fuel in their bodies. We were not rattled by the delay. The girls chatted easily with one another, talking about their social lives and about what they had seen on the track so far. I did my best to engage them, talking about the upcoming race but also joking about silly stuff just to keep their nerves intact.

Mentally, I knew the team was in a great place. We were keen on the task at hand. Our runners were anxious as they continued to ask our coaching staff about race strategy, but with just the right amount of nervous energy, they were ready to execute.

After a couple of hours, we noticed a shift in the Jamaicans. The normal poise and confidence the Jamaicans exuded before the delay began to wane. The temperature dropped by more than twenty degrees, and standard warmup and preparation plans were thrown out the window. Our confidence began to grow with the schedule shake-up, while that of our Caribbean opponents seemed to ebb. I would paraphrase one of my favorite quotes by Martin Luther King Jr. often to the girls and several times before Penn Relays: "The ultimate measure of a person is not where they stand in times of comfort and convenience but where they stand in times of challenge and controversy." (King, 1963) I reminded them that this was one of those challenging and controversial times and that they would be disappointed later in life if they didn't welcome these obstacles.

"Stay devoted mentally and be ready to execute with effort, strategy, and most of all, fight to the finish to the best of your ability," I often said to the girls. They were used to my speeches and my quotes. Whether they realized it or not, they were adopting a mentality more powerful than their physical strength. I prayed that this April day would be the day that both their physical and mental strength would be enough to dethrone the returning Caribbean champions.

CHAPTER 22

MAKING HISTORY

———

We were not the favorite or top ranked team coming into the Penn Relays that year, but on race day, the announcer showed a ton of love to us. Our team came in with an unthinkable mission to capture the school's first Penn Relays Championship of America in the 4x800-meter relay in the afternoon and then come back later in the evening to take a second championship home in the 4x400-meter relay.

Our team had to run one of the fastest twelve times out of the best US and Jamaican teams in the preliminary heats for the 4x800 and one of the top eight times in the 4x400 to make the finals. And all teams had to run a qualifying time at another meet earlier in the season even to earn an invitation to run at Penn Relays. As an appreciation for the American teams, if you crossed the finish line as the first American team in the finals, you were awarded gold Penn Relays watches. As nice as those watches were, I knew we would not feel completely satisfied until we snagged the "Big Penny."

We calculated that it would be too much of a burden for our top runners with two trials races and two final races, so we had to strategize. We prepared eight girls to run the four races and prayed that everyone could carry their weight.

Tashima Stephens and Zawadi Rowe were the most important runners of our first rounds, and they did not disappoint. They ran solid legs during the trial races, allowing two of our top runners to rest their legs for multiple finals the next day. The respective Temple University- and Dartmouth University-bound student athletes gave us the needed depth.

After the rain finally retreated, and after more than two hours delayed, the gun went off for the 4x800-meter finals, and the crowd began to roar! As the race began, the announcer called out the lineup profiling all twelve of the teams and their star performers.

"Ladies and gentlemen, we have the top 800-meter runners in the country vying against the top Jamaican teams! Pope John XXIII has the fastest time from yesterday. This race is wide open. Edwin Allen, Holmwood Tech, Eleanor Roosevelt, Tatnall, Randolph . . ." the announcer continued.

The two powerhouse Jamaican teams, Edwin Allen and Holmwood Tech, used their superior speed and darted out to the lead with our first runner, Dominique Lockhart, tucked in nicely behind. The pace settled into a controlled sprint after the first hundred-meter curve, and all the teams converged on the backstretch. After the first 200 meters, it was a tight twelve-team pack, and the crowd was anxious to see who would make the first bold move. Edwin Allen controlled the pace; we had a hunch they would. But Dominique knew her job was to stay in the race and keep contact with the leaders. For her, it was not a matter of time but of distance. She needed to set the tone for her teammates by letting them know we belonged. By doing that, Dominique could provide the confidence boost her teammates needed.

We prognosticated that some American teams didn't have four strong runners, meaning they couldn't maintain momentum during the entire race. That forced them to put their fastest legs first in the relay to stay in the game as long as possible. We also knew the Jamaican teams would save their fastest two runners for the last two legs but that their first two runners would boast a hefty resume as well. The bottom line: There were no weak links in the Jamaican schools' chains.

Our goal was to run toe-to-toe with the top Jamaican teams and beat them at their own game. We needed a lead off leg with nerves of steel. Dominique, now a junior, would get a bit nervous for the big races, but we could always count on her. She was a running veteran and had plenty of experience since her early DC Redwings days. She had a laid-back disposition and would be willing to make any sacrifice for her teammates. She knew going first would ease the burden and tension on her teammates, and she welcomed the role without hesitation.

Five hundred meters into the race, a few teams had fallen off the lead pack; however, eight teams held on like leaves on a breezy autumn day. Down the backstretch of the track, they all shifted gears and turned on the turbo jets with less than 300 meters left for the first leg. Two American teams took charge, and Dominique held on to a close third. Both Jamaican teams tucked in behind her. The runner from Randolph High School in New Jersey powered her way around the curve and accelerated to another gear to open a gap on second place on the final straightaway before the exchange. The runners from the two Jamaican teams, Holmwood Tech and Edwin Allen, and Dominique followed closely. They were all digging to muster their last bit of energy to give their team the best possible opportunity. Dominique fought her heart out, completing her 800 meters in a strategic two minutes and 16.1 seconds—a personal best—that had us tied for fifth place but only 1.2 seconds off the leader.

In that short period of time, I couldn't help but contemplate: *Did I fully prepare them for this moment? Are we in over our heads?* My stomach was in knots. There had been such a buildup to this moment. Runners, parents, coaches, administrators, and supporters sacrificed to make this happen. The Eleanor Roosevelt girls became local celebrities in the DC area, and now it was their time to prove they were not a fluke. Local newspapers, news stations, and magazines all featured segments on them. *Washington Post* reporters and photographers even attended several practices leading up to the competition. Needless to say, there was an overwhelming amount of pressure to live up to the hype.

Tameka, our second leg, received the baton two strides behind the first-place runner. Dominique had done her job. Tameka immediately showed her gratitude and quickly maneuvered herself into a tie for third and tucked in with the leaders, making it a six-team race. Running a bit wide on the outside of lane two, she positioned herself well to avoid being boxed in.

This was the type of intellect and experience we needed on the second leg, the one that would feature the most jostling and would require the most strategic position to make sure we would maintain contact. Tameka was perfect for the spot. She was our captain and a seasoned runner who moved with poise and confidence in this intense showdown. Tameka was the type of person who would run extra sprints with a teammate who still had more left in their own respective workout. She welcomed work and certainly the pressure. Randolph High School, Tatnall High School from Delaware, Warwick Valley High School from New York, and the usual suspects—Holmwood Tech of Christiana, Jamaica, and Edwin Allen of Clarendon, Jamaica—all clustered in a tight pack, with an additional three teams holding on for dear life. The crowd continued to roar and hung on to this seesaw race every step of the way.

After one quick lap around the oval, the teams began to stretch out, and it was apparent the anticipated three-way race would come to fruition.

"Edwin Allen, Eleanor Roosevelt, and Holmwood Tech are all making a move!" reported the announcer. He continued with a pleasant surprise, adding, "Roosevelt looks like they belong and are taking a shot at the title today!"

It is any kid's dream to hear her name or her team's name called during a race, and you could fully see the adrenaline boost it gave Tameka, encouraging her to make a tough move to crack the race open into a three-way stampede with Holmwood and Edwin Allen. At that point, it was evident she wasn't concerned with who was the fastest but instead wanted to see who had the most guts. She wanted to make sure her two premier Jamaican opponents weren't running comfortably on the backstretch, saving for a strong kick. So, she continued to push the pace, forcing the Jamaican teams to go with her.

With 200 meters to go, Tameka kicked into high gear and surged past her Jamaican competitors, and they countered and responded. First, the Holmwood runner moved with her, and then Edwin Allen's runner eventually joined the party with a delayed move. In the fight down the homestretch, as she moved toward her teammate waving her arm, almost impatiently waiting to grab the baton, Tameka powered through the last hundred meters of her leg, holding off the two Jamaicans and handing off in a three-way tie with a 2:14.5 split.

Tameka handed off the baton to her teammate Marika Walker, our two-time Maryland cross country state champion. At the same time, Edwin Allen's third leg waited too late to get out as her teammate approached, which caused the two of them to fumble the baton in the exchange. Marika took advantage of this falter and immediately established her dominance. She took the lead after the first hundred meters as she entered the backstretch. She established a quick first 400 meters and didn't let her competitors breathe comfortably or relax. Edwin Allen's runner recovered quickly from the botched exchange, and the three became company again, with a chase pack a bit off the pace but still hanging around. Marika attempted to separate from the two Jamaican runners with her beautiful and gazelle-like strides, but they hung on for dear life. The announcer called out Marika's name and began to list our team's resume and accomplishments.

"Eleanor Roosevelt High School did the inconceivable, winning the indoor nationals in this race, the 4x200-meter relay, the 4x400-meter relay, and the distance medley relay, and is currently in the lead!"

Holmwood Tech's runner countered Marika's move with 350 meters to go, but Marika held on and relied on her cross country strength to power through. Edwin Allen's runner couldn't close the gap, and it appeared it would be a two-team race. With 150 meters to go, Keno Heaven of Holmwood surged forward and broke away a little bit. But just as they rounded the final turn, Marika made a late push down the final straightaway. Keno's muscles began to tighten up with thirty meters to go, sensing she still had company by the sound of the crowd. Marika dug in to shave the lead, stopping her split in a personal record of 2:10.8, and we were back handing off the baton at the same time. The crowd was hanging over the rails in awe.

Tasha Stanley had a tall order as our anchor, facing off against superstar and future Jamaican Olympian Bobby-Gaye Wilkins. Although the odds were not in our favor, there was no doubt in our minds that Tasha would give it a valiant effort. Tasha was a fierce competitor and always left it all on the track. Bobby-Gaye instantly took charge, but Tasha did not succumb to the relentless pace and drafted on Bobby-Gaye's shoulder for the first 400 meters. At this point, the thirty-nine-thousand-plus people in attendance were cheering at a deafening decibel.

"Tasha Stanley of Roosevelt is making a run for the win. The national record is in jeopardy. Bobby-Gaye is still in the lead!" the announcer reported to the crowd.

Tasha knew the plan was to make Bobby-Gaye run the next 200 meters honestly. This was our strategy: Make your opponent run every step of the way! We studied the Jamaican style of racing relentlessly, and one common strategy they used was to cruise during the third 200 meters of the 800-meter race, then regroup for the last 150 to 200 meters, using their pure speed and strength.

So, Tasha made her opponent work, but Bobby-Gaye stayed composed, striding easily and relaxed, still making it look effortless. With 150 meters left in the race, Bobby-Gaye surged again, and this time it was to put Tasha away for good. Coming onto the final straightaway with less than one hundred meters to go, Bobby-Gaye had a ten-meter cushion on Tasha. The Jamaican flags were blazing and the whistles howling. Just as they began to celebrate, Tasha put her head down and began to unleash her kick. We had done many sprints at the end of critical workouts to simulate this moment, and no doubt about it—she was prepared. But sometimes in life, you come across people who are just more talented, more hungry, and faster. With fifty meters to go, Stanley was matching Bobby-Gaye's stride and speed, but it appeared to be too late.

Then, with thirty meters to go, Bobby-Gaye began to look uncomfortable. Her shoulders lifted in tightness and her face appeared strained as she tried to hold her ferocious finish just as Tasha was inching closer to her. With twenty meters left, the lead was trimmed down to five meters, and it became an unbelievable showdown, causing the Americans in the stadium to erupt. Chants of "USA! USA!" echoed vigorously as the momentum shifted our way.

The lead was down to three meters with a mere ten meters left in the race, and although Bobby-Gaye was strong, her muscles were also tight and tired, and her stride began to close. I was confident in the fact that Tasha would finish. The eighty-meter accelerations at the end of tough workouts, simulating control of the rate of deceleration, were actually working.

Tasha pulled up side-by-side with Bobby, and they crossed the finish line in a photo finish. A hush came over the crowd, and all eyes went to the scoreboard to validate the outcome. Holmwood Tech's name was posted first, but all teams were not tabulated. In a quick flash, Eleanor Roosevelt's name appeared at the top of the scoreboard. Our time beat theirs by four hundredths of a second!

The crowd went absolutely insane! Tasha was barely able to walk, and her teammates ran to her aid. She wobbled, looking dazed, as if she had been in a fight for her life. Her teammates held her up as they pumped their fists in the air, knowing this was their day.

"Eleanor Roosevelt has done it! What a race! Tasha Stanley, come-from-the-back anchor, finishes in a blistering 2:09, the fastest split of the day."

I raced from my coaching spot near the 200-meter mark on the other side of the stadium, through the tunnel under the stadium and onto the field. I met my girls in the infield and gave them a huge hug. I was sweating, my heart was pounding, and I was grinning from ear to ear. I couldn't believe it.

"Yes! Yes!" I continued to shout. I posed for pictures and paused for more hugs and high-fives from field officials and a few friends who had also made their way to the finish line. *We did it! We actually beat the Jamaicans!*

Our girls took a victory lap with the American flag and took countless proud photos afterward. Last but not least, our girls were awarded the "Big Penny." The quartet hoisted it over their heads. It took all four of them, fatigued, to lift a plaque of that weight and magnitude. What an unbelievable moment for the girls, for our country, and for me.

While we were ecstatic about the 4x800-meter relay victory, we knew what we went there to do—bring home two "Big Pennies" by also beating the Jamaicans in the 4x400-meter relay, the last race of the day and the last race of the meet for high school girls' teams. If we could accomplish that mission, we would make history by being the first US team to do so. After a quick celebration, we went to rally around the four girls who would represent us in the 4x400-meter relay final.

Tameka and Tasha from the 4x800 would join Tameka's twin sister, Takecia, and Doris Anyawu for the finals. Tashima Stephens gave us an amazing leg in the 4x400 trials to secure our position for the final. Again, the odds were stacked against us. Bobby-Gaye Wilkins returned to the

Jamaican lineup, and she had major help from her all-star teammates, plus a chip on her shoulder. The Holmwood Tech team added Anastasia Le-Roy to its quartet. Anastasia was a powerful runner and went on to represent her country at the 2019 world championships in Doha, Qatar, and other prominent world class competitions once she graduated from high school. (World Athletics, 2019) (GC2018, 2018)

We had about three hours between the end of the 4x400 and the start of the 4x800 final. The girls who would have to run again cooled down with a light ten-minute jog in the infield, then rejoined the rest of the team in the stands. They refueled with mango slices, granola bars, and a slice of wheat bread while making sure to stay off their feet to let their legs rest. Before we knew it, it was time to head back down to the warmup area for our last race of the day.

As we warmed up in the community turf field shared by a slew of other teams, I noticed other runners and coaches looking our way. I could hear the whispers, "That's them. They're the team that beat them," and, "I can't believe they beat them." My favorite was, "They're in trouble now. The Jamaicans will be out for revenge."

During their entire warmup, other runners eyed our girls, watching them carefully, sizing them up to determine how our girls accomplished such a feat. They were also trying to discern whether we could do it again or whether it was just a fluke. A few coaches and runners actually approached the girls and me and gave us high-fives and kudos for our 4x800 victory. I could tell our girls began to grow uncomfortable with the attention and just wanted to focus on their fast-approaching next race.

"Come on, ladies. Let's move over here," I called out. I moved them to a more remote area to finish their warmup.

As we rounded a collection of trees, we spotted the Holmwood team, tucked away with their entourage of runners, coaches, and massage therapists, preparing for the final race. I kept my eyes focused on my team, leading them through the rest of their warmup routine, working earnestly to hide the stirring nerves that were having a field day in the pit of my belly.

As we made our way to the bullpen to check in for the race and to receive final instructions from race officials, I called the girls in for one last, quick huddle before they moved to an area off limits to coaches. I took a steady breath and looked at each of them before I said, "Ladies, this has been an amazing journey. It's not about any medals or trophies or awards. You've done a heck of a job this season. The love and appreciation you've shown your teammates and your coaches, that's what counts! We're family, and we've learned so much along the way. Let's go out here and leave it all on the track. Trust your training, trust your strategy, and most of all, trust one another. Now, hands in. Lady Raiders on three and family on six!"

"One, two, three . . . Lady Raiders!" the girls replied. "Four, five, six . . . Family!" they all said in unison. They embraced each other tightly, turned, and headed to the bullpen to line up at the starting line. *Here we go again. One more chance,* I thought as I took another deep breath to try and calm my raging stomach.

As the first legs lined up on their respective starting lines, camera flashes popped from all over the stadium. *Pow!* The gun went off, and the crowd jumped to its feet again. I'm sure most spectators believed there would be a reckoning forthcoming after the 4x800.

Our indomitable and spirited sophomore, Doris Anyawu, who would later run for Penn State, was our lead-off runner.

She did not disappoint with her one-lap sprint. She hugged the line as closely as possible on the curves without touching them to minimize her distance and powered her way to a 56.7-second split. Doris brought the baton in with the leading pack and handed off to the experienced senior captain Tameka.

Tameka again ran the strategic second leg, which involved some jostling and maneuvering after the first turn as runners broke from their lanes to position themselves in the inside lanes. In a tight pack, Tameka was tied for third and a couple of steps off the leader. She made a bold and tough move on the last turn that positioned her in fourth, allowing her to swing to the outside and create space to get around the other US team, Boys and Girls High of New York. The race was playing out just like the 4x800. Holmwood, in their maroon singlets, opened up a few strides to separate from us and Edwin Allen, in their baby blue uniforms. Tameka charged into the exchange zone, neck and neck with Edwin Allen and just a few steps behind Holmwood in the blazin' time of 54.5 seconds.

Tasha grabbed the baton and bolted out as our third leg. It was a five-team race after the first 200 meters, with two US teams and three Jamaican teams. A third Jamaican team, St. Jago, scratched and clawed its way into the race and was just off Tasha's heels. As St. Jago made its move and Boys and Girls dropped off the pace, Stanley felt the pressure and accelerated into first place in the last ten meters of her leg, handing off the baton after a 54.7-second split.

Just when the Americans in the crowd began to celebrate, Edwin Allen darted past Tameka's twin sister Takecia, who was our fourth and final leg. Holmwood gradually inched its way next to Takecia and nudged past her on the final turn. Now in third place with one hundred meters to go,

Takecia repositioned herself to the outside of the leaders. Eighty meters to go now. Holmwood took the lead, and for a split second, it looked as if it would be a one-two Jamaican finish. But Takecia would not go down without a fight. She kept her composure with one final surge, closing the gap between her and her international competitors. Sixty meters. Neck and neck, then it was over. The Holmwood and Edwin Allen anchor legs had nothing left. They could not respond to Takecia's surge. Takecia pulled away in the final meters and hoisted both arms in the air as she crossed the finish line. She ran a blistering 53.5 seconds. She and her teammates captured their second "Big Penny" of the day!

This time, I decided not to sprint all the way through the tunnel to reach the girls in the infield near the finish line. *We did it! No way! We did it!* I thought before I hopped down the ten-foot wall of the stadium separating the spectator seats from the track. Two track officials glared at me, but when they saw the jubilation on my face and recognized my team gear, they refrained from reprimanding me and looked the other way. I made it down with our other coaches to the infield, giving high-fives to familiar faces along the way. As I approached the finish line, I embraced the girls, grinning, hugging, and jumping as we celebrated this unbelievable feat. We made American high school sports history. We became the first US team to win two relays against the Jamaicans at one Penn Relays Carnival. This special group of runners learned the true essence of what the sport of running could offer on that day and beyond. They gave every ounce of effort for themselves and for one another, day in and day out. And they welcomed the challenges and adversities, embracing the process to face their fears, doubts, and insecurities to evolve and reveal better versions of themselves. Against all odds, we ran, and we prevailed. Together.

EPILOGUE

As I log my two-thousandth mile during our 2020–21 COVID-19 pandemic, I reflect on the dynamic relationship I have had with running. Though I enjoyed other sports more than running at times, running undoubtedly has done more for me than all other sports combined. In spite of the sheer agony and pain that comes with running, it has opened doors for me throughout life. Most of all, it opened me up to who I am as a person. It revealed to me my potential and capabilities, and I will always be grateful for that. When my emotions were pulling me into a dark hole, running got me through the tough times at home, the dyslexia in school, the lack of confidence, and the lack of clarity I had in life. Running taught me to persevere, through uncertainty, through depression, through relationship challenges. I am not me without running. This is why I have been so passionate to inspire others through this sport and to push everyone I come into contact with to be the best version of themselves regardless of the odds against them. I will always be appreciative of the 2007 Lady Raiders for allowing me to reach that pinnacle with them. They taught me to be patient, and they taught me to believe in myself as a coach and most of all, as a person.

That year, the girls didn't stop their dominance at the Penn Relays. They went on to win the Maryland 4A outdoor track and field championships, taking gold in the 200 meters, 3,200 meters, 300-meter hurdles and the 4x800-meter relay. They then went on to win the highly coveted 4x400 and 4x800 relay titles at the New Balance High School National Outdoor Championship, where they also broke the Sprint Medley national record with a 3:51 first-place finish. Takecia ran an amazing 52-second split on the 400-meter leg, and Marika sealed the deal with a 2:06 closing split on the final 800-meter leg.

Tasha Stanley was named the high school relay performer of the meet at the 2007 Penn Relays. She returned to the meet the following year and was awarded the same honor. In 2008, she was on the 4x800-meter relay that averaged 2:10 per runner and shattered the US high school record by seven seconds, along with Dominique Lockhart, Brittany Ogunmokun, and freshman Amirah Johnson. As anchor leg, she captured another championship title in the 4x400-meter relay with Afia Charles, Elan Hilare, and Doris Anyawu.

Tasha, the Jameson twins Tameka and Takecia, and Dominque were integral members of those history-making relay teams in 2007. They all continued competing in college and had formidable collegiate running careers. Tasha went on to run for the University of North Carolina at Chapel Hill. The Jameson twins ran at the University of Miami. And Dominique competed for Mississippi State University.

After that amazing Penn Relays ride, I ventured into collegiate coaching in the fall of 2008 at the University of Maryland, and after a four-year stint, I realized my love for high school running was undeniable. I returned to high school coaching in 2012 and am still there, loving every minute of it. It's where I got my start as a runner and where I will always be grateful.

I still keep in contact with so many of the runners I coached on the Eleanor Roosevelt team and all the teams I've coached in the past, and I have enjoyed the decades-long relationships we've established. I've attended their college graduations and weddings. I've celebrated their milestones and successes as new parents. And I've even mentored some as blossoming running coaches themselves. That victorious day in 2007 at Penn Relays will remain one of the most memorable moments in my life. But the satisfaction of seeing runners I've coached take what they've learned from running and apply it to the next phases of their lives in a way that positively impacts others is what makes me feel most proud. My greatest reward is when they've learned that there will always be odds to face, and they keep running anyway.

ACKNOWLEDGMENTS

Thank you.

I want to start by saying thank you to those who went on my personal journey with me and read this memoir.

Thank you to my mom for trusting me with her personal stories and cheering me on along the way.

To my beautiful wife, Jami Dunham, who has been my inspiration and strength with all the long hours and sacrifices. And to Nia, Niles, and my Wilson and Dunham families for being my village. Special thanks to my siblings Nicole Dunham, Deneen Dunham, Darin Dunham, and Preston Dunham.

To my Gary Vohr, Tolleston, Horace Mann community, and childhood friends who gave me many fond memories and balanced any odds that I faced.

To my Howard University administrators, professors, classmates, and community for shaping and molding me into who I am today. I wouldn't have this story without you.

To the fierce Lady Raiders: Thank you for the memorable seasons and moments, those in this book and beyond. I treasure the lifelong bonds we all share.

To Hannah Tropf and Under Armour Running for your continued support in all of my endeavors.

To Desmond Williams and Nylinka School Solutions for being the spark I needed to embark on this writing journey.

To my illustrious marketing team of consultants: Megan Laurent, Simone Hunter, Branded by Simone, Thelma Ortega, Kelly Bedrossian, and Bedro Brand Box.

To Professor Koester, Aislyn Gilbert, Jessica Fleischman, Linda Berardelli, and Lauren Sweeney: Thank you for guidance, expertise, and encouragement to put my story out into the world.

To Aunt Delores Hildreth, Aunt Barbara Washington, Aunt Glen Dunham, Aunt Tommie Cockrell, Aunt Shirley, Uncle Hank Dunham, Tiffany Wells, Brett Allen, Joey Gibbs, Steve Powell, Connie Williams, Eric Smoot, Phil Mckenzie, Carson Edwards, Jomo Davis, and Shaun Bell: Your love, reassurance, and willingness to share your stories made this possible.

To NDP staff: Thank you for making this book a reality and working with me, hand in hand.

To past professors, teachers, mentors, and coaches who always encouraged me: Thank you for seeing what you did in me. It still means the world today. Special thanks to Roosevelt "Chief" Pulliam and William P. Moultrie, who saw the potential in me before I saw it in myself.

To my awesome coaching staffs who always supported our mission and made the journey that much more enjoyable:

Eleanor Roosevelt Coaching Staff

DC Redwings Coaching Staff

Special shout out to the brothers of Alpha Phi Alpha Fraternity, Incorporated, Beta Chapter, and my track and field and cross country brothers from Gary, Horace Mann, and Howard University.

To my amazing beta readers, thank you for your time and valuable feedback during my writing process:

Scott Silverstein	Tiffany Wells
Lonice Priester	Kelli McCrary
Jesse Meyer	Gaby Grebski
Myra Tanamor	Mindy Galoob
Nicole Dunham	Stephen Galoob

To all those who supported my presale campaign:

Angela Senior	Dave Powell
The Grannis Family	Maximillian Lindenberg
The Rowland Family	Rachel McNinch
The Loughran Family	Paul McKay
The Brennan Family	Brian Smith
Salvatore Caccavale	Zack Riegel
Michel Martin	Antonio Toppin
Glen and Hank Dunham	Mitch Gore
Ronald Sullivan	Felicia Johnson
Kevin Thompson	Kyle Graves
Katherine Loughran	Jennifer Conklin
Veronica Salcido	Ashley McMaster
Jessica Neal	Susan Coates
Drew Watkins	Cranston Gittens
Wali Lathan	Betty Anderson
Tanesha Francis	Cynthia Cheatham
Dr. Bill Wooden	Jane Kruszewski
Rodney Greene	Edward P. Lee
Theresa Stattel	Nicole Chamberlain
Maurice Dukes	Dan Israel
Vic Montgomery	Josh Wright
Curtis Kidd Telemaque	Thelma Hale
Allyceia Brinkley	Kylie A. Ritz

Jennifer Kaczor
Angela Roberson
Martha McIntosh
Anthony Dozier
Monique Ross
Brandon Wims
The Kovner Family
Jason Guyton
Matt Green
Eugene V. Hildebrand III
Mary Ann Akers
Yodit Tefera
Brenda Harris
Delores Hildreth
Sarah O'Herron
Givon Conner
Susana Sitja
Tina Maxwell
Vic Montgomery
Beatriz Cuartas
Tracie Tillery
David Yulfo
Paul Gotzman
Ronee Jarman
Catherine Ann Penafiel
Dennis Lattmann
Gabriel Smith
Deana Jordan Sullivan
Bridget Nolan
Patricia D Milikin
Linda Blake
Min Kelsey-Levine

William Heinle
Erin Doherty
Lizabeth Coppock
Yolanda Lockwood
Pamela Brandon
Wendel Dunham
Myron Abston
Dondre Simpson
Seann Pelkey
Roger Collins
Alfred McMurray
Michael King Jr.
Nnenna Oluigbo
Ivette Dominguez
David R. Jefferson
Kristin Regen
Heather Jeff
Jason Jackson
Andrea Haywood
Kathleen Carroll
Mindy Galoob
Marlon Cohen
Julia Tillman
Camille Sabbakhan
Bernard Oliver
Preston Dunham
Sean and Tangela Parran
Martill Seymour
Aaron Coates
Tashima Stephens
Chaka Long
Yuliana Haworth

Bardell Brown
Kwame Bailey
Sheri Carline
Anna Gregory
Kenyan McDuffie
Kit Arrington
LaNysha Foss
Bernie Sisk
Lonice Priester
Courtney Clark
Iftikhar Khan
Bobby Caballero
Gwendolyn L. Wiggins
Brandon Osazuwa
Juan C. Abreu
Ashley Seymour
Bill Kappenhagen
Leslie Thompson
Don Smith
Arielle Statham
Phillip Kang
Lois Wilkins
Nathaniel Metts
Julio A. Castillo
Benny Morgan
Carolyn Papetti
Marius Morgan
Tyree Newman
Sellano Simmons
Tamlin Antoine
Rafford Seymour
Brent Collier

Oscar Ortega
Darrick Coleman
Marvin Graves
Marcus Scott
Marvin Parker
James P. Washington
Luca Pedone
Anita Jones
Rebecca Maltzman
Stratton Penberthy
Prabhleen Lamba
Zawadi Rowe
Brian Kobil
Neal Downing
Deborah Lincoln
Leslie Chappelle
Charyn Clark
Mona Luddy Benach
Chinelo Y. Cambron
Tiffany Wells
Michael McCoy
Jim Hagberg
Patrice Jones
Tommie Cockrell
Tanya Washington
Marvin Lester
Kira Tewalt
Shirley Ann Harris
Florence Harth Carter
Kelly Cole
Francesca Mason
Shana E. Bailey

Keith Dix

Cole Randolph

Carl Dear

Zacch Olorunnipa

Diana Blitz

Erwin Baylor

Kelli McCrary

Sarah Howard

Lauren Krasnodembski

Tia Clemmons

Urana Joseph

Shunda Adams

Paula Whitfield

Donald Harrison

Catherine Skibo

Medgar A. Webster, Sr.

Mathis Banks

Timothy McMahon

Ariana Tabatabaie

Monica Mosley

Andrea Moody

Tiffany Moore

Marcel Virachittevin

Karen Dennis

Elizabeth Striebel

Marybeth Snyder

Linda Ertz

Brett Allen

Alexis Geier Horan

Zoe Vidaurre

Michael Reives

Prasad Gerard

DaNa Carlis

Gabrielle Chappelle

Sarath K. Nadella

Ayanna Mackins

Sabrina Davis

Mandi L. Smith

Yasemin Washington

Tara LaCroix

Richelle Sitton

Anne Charles

Asinia Crawford

Darren E. Foster

Meisha Abbasinejad

Russell Drake

Laura Gonzalez

Roy Austin

Cynthia Mattison

Christine Carroll

Brian Yourish

Ni-Ann Cross

Carlos Pla

Godelinde Degroot

Moira Hayward

Siprenia Pearson

Kesha Frisby

Charles Chappelle

Allie O'Brien

Kathleen Harris

Janie Davis

Hank Dunham

Dineen James

Felicia Binion Williams

Lee Bruner
Josh Finkle
Beverly Riley
Karen Dunham
Margaret Knight
Sam Frumkin
Sean T. Coleman
Brittany Ogunmokun
Ransom Miller
Myla Scott
Kenny Dudley
Cheryl Fox
Brian Dunham
Mark McCants
Avery Taylor
Charles Graham
Nicole Banker
Amy Boris
Gerry Gretschel
Harper Randolph
Curtis Whittaker
Simona Gerhardt
Kim Elliott Banks
Daniel De Lude
Marilyn Fossberg
Kathy Dalby
Eileen Langholtz
Kevin Engram
Susan Toth
Dino Anders
Jasmine T. Riley
Leota Bowen

Marika Walker
Helen Ruggiero
Nicole Dunham-Watkins
Jim Gerstein
Kathleen Murray
Sara Peczkowski
Victor Blackett
Michael Lemon
Vennard Wright
Matt Dernoga
Kathryn Blanchard
Brendan Quinn
Arielle Banks
Jennifer Conklin
Sara Peczkowski
Becky Yep
Teshika Rivers
Pandelis Margaronis
Sara Tobin
David Harris
Pamela Gordon
Jason Smith
Derek Woelfel
Gregory Bargeman
Anna Cestari
Marc Luchtefeld
Kirsten Keefe
Lauren E. Case
Gaby Grebski
Lydia Colon
Marci M. Matthews
Stephen Hays

Helen Dooley

Earl Skrine

Amy Suardi

Leah Skrine

Katya Svirina

Brandy Maes

Kevin Jenkins

Jesse Lauritsen

Eric Koester

Thomase Dibiase

Teddy Atcherson

Delicia Dunham

Rose Rakas

Jill Laing

Shomari Jennings

Darnice Cloudy

London Lawson

Cranston Gittens

Mathis Banks

Matthew Comas

Lola Fashina

Terence Edgerson

APPENDIX

AUTHOR'S NOTE

Sloan, Paul, Penny Roberts (contrib.), and William Recktenwald (contrib.). "Gary Takes over as Murder Capital of US." *Chicago Tribune.* January 3, 1994. https://www.chicagotribune.com/news/ct-xpm-1994-01-03-9401030009-story.html.

CHAPTER 5

Bullet. "Horace Mann High School." *Autopsy of Architecture* (blog). June 21, 2021. https://autopsyofarchitecture.com/horace-mann-high-school/.

Davich, Jerry. *Lost Gary, Indiana.* Mount Pleasant, SC: Arcadia Publishing, 2015.

CHAPTER 9

Biography.com Editors. "Charles Drew Biography." The Biography.com website. Last modified September 3, 2020. Accessed March 3, 2021. https://www.biography.com/scientist/charles-drew.

Glubb, John Bagot, and Ass'ad Sulaiman Abdo. "Mecca." *Encyclopedia Britannica.* February 15, 2021. https://www.britannica.com/place/Mecca.

Office for Civil Rights (OCR). "Historically Black Colleges and Universities and Higher Education Desegregation." US Department of Education. January 3, 1991. Last modified January 10, 2021. https://www2.ed.gov/about/offices/list/ocr/docs/hq9511.html.

CHAPTER 10

Alpha Phi Alpha Fraternity, Inc. "Our History." Accessed May 10, 2021. https://apa1906.net/our-history/.

US Department of Commerce. Bureau of the Census. 1990 Census of Population General Population Characteristics Indiana. Washington DC, 22 April 1992. Superintendent of Documents, US Government Printing Office. https://www2.census.gov/library/publications/decennial/1990/cp-1/cp-1-16.pdf.

US Track and Field and Cross Country Coaches Association
(USTFCCCA). "Bill Moultrie, USTFCCCA Coaches Hall of
Fame, Class of 2006." Accessed December 2, 2020.
http://www.ustfccca.org/awards/bill-moultrie-ustfccca-
class-of-2006.

CHAPTER 14

History.com Editors. "Apartheid." History. Updated March 3,
2020.
https://www.history.com/topics/africa/apartheid.

CHAPTER 18

Swindoll, Charles R. "Charles R. Swindoll: Quotes." Goodreads.
Accessed May 10, 2021.
https://www.goodreads.com/author/quotes/5139.Charles_R_
Swindoll.

CHAPTER 19

Flynn, Sean P. "Roosevelt Still Has Catching Up to Do." *The
Washington Post*. April 28, 2006.
https://www.washingtonpost.com/wp-dyn/content/
article/2006/04/27/AR2006042702426.html.

National High School Track and Field Hall of Fame (NHS T&F
HOF). "Don Norford." The National Scholastic Athletics
Foundation. Accessed June 25, 2021.
https://nationalhighschooltrackandfieldhof.org/showcase/
don-norford/.

Olympic Games. "Bobby-Gaye Wilkins: Olympic Results Beijing 2008." Updated August 2008. Accessed May 10, 2021. https://olympics.com/en/athletes/bobby-gaye-wilkins#b2p-athlete-olympic-results.

Penn Relays. "2007 Results by Level: High School Girls." Accessed May 10, 2021. http://pennrelaysonline.com/History/schedule.aspx?l=HSG.

CHAPTER 21

King, Jr., Martin Luther. *Strength to Love.* New York: Harper & Row, 1963.

CHAPTER 22

Gold Coast 2018 XXI Commonwealth Games (GC2018). "Participants: Anastasia Le-Roy." Updated April 2018. Accessed May 10, 2021. https://results.gc2018.com/en/athletics/athlete-profile-n6032691-anastasia-le-roy.htm.

Penn Relays. "2007 Results by Level: High School Girls." Accessed May 10, 2021. http://pennrelaysonline.com/History/schedule.aspx?l=HSG.

World Athletics. "Jamaica Announces Team for IAAF World Athletics Championships Doha 2019." World Athletics News. September 12, 2019. https://www.worldathletics.org/news/news/jamaica-world-championships-doha-2019.